CHRONICLES

Stories of Faith, Fear and Fortitude

Volume.1

Stories of Faith, Fear
and Fortitude

Volume.1

JAI STONE

and 10 Ambassadors of Emotional Nudity

HER CHRONICLES
Stories of Faith, Fear and Fortitude, Volume 1

Copyright © 2015 Jai Stone

Published By: Stone Angel Press – Atlanta, GA

Editor: Carla DuPont

Author Photo Taken By: Amadi Phillips

Book Cover and Interior Layout: Purposely Created Publishing

ISBN-13: 978-0-9966942-0-9 (paperback)
ISBN-13: 978-0-9966942-1-6 (e-book)

Special discounts are available on bulk quantity purchases by book clubs, associations and special interest groups. For details email: jai@jaistone.com

DEDICATION

Everyone has a story, but most of us are not brave enough to share our deepest thoughts and feelings. We are far too worried about the painful judgments and too afraid of the emotions that we have hidden for many years.

This anthology is dedicated to all the women like Maya Angelou and Brene Brown who have found the courage to share, and to the ladies who will discover their courage while reading this book.

Lastly, I want to dedicate this collaboration to the women who came before us who never had the opportunity to share their stories. To all these women, I applaud you and I am humbled by your presence.

TABLE OF CONTENTS

TABLE OF CONTENTS •

ACKNOWLEDGEMENTS

I am eternally grateful to the Almighty God for giving me the message, talents, voice, and courage to carry out my calling according to His will. It is my calling to be an obedient vessel in His service.

To my parents, Daisy Beckham Wright *(deceased 2002)* and Russell L. Wright, Sr. *(deceased 2015)* who made it their life's mission to ensure I had every opportunity to succeed; and at the very least, I was strong enough to survive any storm. Any courage that I may exude is a result of my Mom's tireless dedication to making me live a life without fear or regrets, and my Dad's insistence that I NEVER give up!

Thanks to my siblings who accept me, and all my crap with very little complaining (most days), and a whole lot of love (always). Jocelyn, R.L., Zita, and Rhonda thanks for being the consummate support system that just happens to share my DNA. And, my nieces Alyssa and Sauyer who bring me the purest form of joy!

Thanks to my friends who INSISTED that I write this book! Thanks for cheering me on, telling me the terrible truth, and kicking my ass all the way to the finish line. Aprille Franks Hunt, Mairo Akpose Simpson, Akilah Richards, Timothy Roberts, Joy Warren, Lamar Tyler, Charles Major Charli Penn, Richard 'Big Rich' Evans, and Jack A. Daniels.

Thanks to my SisterFriends who supported me through the tough sh*t mentioned in this book: Melanie Richardson, Nadia Armstrong, Tretta Bush, Leida Speller, Tana Gilmore, Donna Purvis, Patrice Hector and Shannon White.

Thanks to my co-authors who invested tireless resources into this project without complaints or gripes. I am so humbled by the faith they had in me. Thank you: Becky, Brandi, DeVay, Felicia, Malla, Meochia, Talisha, Tameka W., Tomika B., and T. Renee.

Special thanks to Team Jai who pulled this whole thing together. Necie Black, Twanna Gill, Tieshena Davis, and Carla DuPont.

To my readers, fans and followers, I am grateful that you find value in my message. I am honored that you have embraced me, and humbled each time you support me. Please know that you are greatly appreciated.

INTRODUCTION

*T*here is something wonderfully spectacular that happens when a group of amazing women come together for a cause, and this anthology is no exception. I have been an entrepreneur for nearly 14 years, and I have had the honor and privilege to have many clients share their deepest most painful and most triumphant stories with me, and I thought that it was about time for me to encourage some those women to share these stories with the world.

As you read each co-author's story, you will find yourself experiencing a full range of emotions moving from joy, to sadness, to fear, then anger, and even triumph. You will find similarities in the stories of some women and others will resemble your own tale. But, what you will find most is the common thread spun between faith, fear and fortitude.

When I question women about their resilience, they usually give credit to an external source, the source where their faith lies. I am a firm believer that we must believe in something bigger than ourselves in order to walk in our divine purpose. That's FAITH!

When I sat with these women and learned about their choices, they often shied away from confrontation, unpleasant memories, or circumstances that left them vulnerable. As I began to dig into their "why's," I came to the conclusion that often FEAR keeps us from being whole.

But what struck me most was how many women have gone forward to accomplish considerable personal and professional success, despite previous circumstances. And THAT is the FORTITUDE that will make your soul scream YES!!

It is my honor to collaborate with 10 amazing women, who were courageous enough to share their stories of faith, fear and fortitude.

I humbly salute these Ambassadors of Emotional Nudity.

Why Is She So Fat? My Secret Journey from Self Hate to Celebrity Status

JAI STONE

● ●

hy is she so fat? It's a question that many people have in their head when they first lay eyes on me. Most people don't have the audacity to say it out loud, but I can always tell based on their comments or behavior. There is the standard back-handed compliment "you have such a pretty FACE"; a statement that clearly indicates that my beauty does not extend below the waist. Some others are much bolder with statements like "if you'd just lose weight, you would be gorgeous."

I've certainly heard the question enough times over the years, so let's just start with the obvious here. Yes, I am overweight. I'm not talking 15 or 20 vanity pounds; I am, without a doubt, obese. I have struggled with weight since I was a teenager and it is still a daily challenge for me.

3

And, with all of the success I've had in almost every arena of my life, it's the one area where I have yet to find a winning solution. I am officially part of the obesity epidemic that plagues America.

Now, I could give you a long drawn out story about all the health issues and personal challenges that have contributed to my problem but all of that would sound like excuses, and I make none of those. I will say that food is my coping mechanism and I have needed to cope with a lot in my life. But again, I'm not making excuses; I'm simply sharing my reasons with you.

SWAN DIVE! My Ugly Duckling Phase

But believe it or not, I wasn't always fat. I don't know exactly when I became overweight, but I know that sometime around middle school folks started to treat me differently. As a kid I was never considered 'pretty', that acclaim came much later in life. My childhood friends often said "your sisters look better than you" or "wow, your best friend is REALLY pretty." But no such compliments ever flowed in my direction.

In high school, is when I started to get those back-handed compliments like boys saying "I would holla at you if you were a little slimmer" or teachers saying "you are so smart, but you are just too big for your age". Then there was Mrs. Pat who did my hair and single handedly kept me in Gheri Curls until I was in college. I will never forget the Thursday evening when she sat me down in her kitchen and told me that if I wanted to get a man, I would need to work on losing weight. "No man wants to pick you up in his two-seater with you weighing down one side of the car" she said in a matter of fact tone, all the while looking me dead in my eyes. I just nodded and agreed with her. So by the time I was in my 20s I came to firmly believe that I was simply passable, provided a man could look past my weight.

There were a few times in my life where I found the occasional validation. Like the summer I spent in Europe and I discovered that Italian men couldn't get enough of me. I was flattered an overwhelmed by all the attention. Back in the states, being brown and round was NOT at all a combination of beauty elements that stopped traffic. Yet here I was in a foreign country being pursued like some sort of supermodel.

I also remember being in the night club one night with 3 friends and we were dead set on "getting the party started". We had all taken notice of the man who was arguably the finest dude in the club. He strolled around the club and peacocked and perched from one post to the next with all the women in the club keeping a close eye on him. Then the DJ must have decided it was time to "slow jam" because he started playing some Jodeci and the entire mood of the club shifted. The hunky, handsome dude sat his drink on the bar and headed across the dance floor where the 4 of us were standing. Several sets of eyes followed him as he made his journey across the dance floor, I think everyone wanted to see who he would "choose" as his partner.

As Mr. Fabulous drew closer to where my crew was standing, we started to whisper to each other "girrrrlll here he comes, here he comes"! At this point I was accustomed to being the odd man out, so I turned to my friends so I could watch their reaction when he asked one of them to dance. I could feel him approaching, but I never looked at him, I didn't want to miss watching one of my friends snag the hottest dude in the club. I heard him say "excuse me pretty lady, but would you like to dance." I peered closely at my friends with slight confusion because none of them were responding to this man's question. Then he asked again, "excuse me, would you like to dance." Suddenly all 3 of my friends turned to look at me with a sense of alarm in their eyes.

Then Michelle said "Jayyyyy, he's talking to you." I abruptly turned and looked at Mr. Fabulous and found him staring at me. In that moment I sunk into a deeper layer of confusion and I said "oh wait, are you talking to me?!" He responded, "yes, pretty lady... would you dance with me." I stared for another second then said "sure". And with that he took my hand and led me slowly and deliberately to the edge of the dance floor where he turned and pulled me close to him then started to sway. I could feel all the cold stares from other women hitting me like daggers and I must have stiffened my body, because he pulled me slightly closer and leaned down and whispered in my ear "relax, I got you." Woooooo weee! I swear I could have swooned and passed out like Miss Erma when she caught the holy ghost errrry weekend at church.

I remember seeing my girlfriends on the side of the dance floor, who had all moved to get a better look and me and Mr. Fabulous. They were elbowing each other, whispering, giggling and waving at me like 3 teenagers at the school dance. When my handsome capture finally released me, he said "thank you for the dance lady" and then took my hand and walked me back over to my friends. Ahhh, but that's not all! Every time the DJ went into slow jam mode my bulky boo returned to ask me to dance again. I was the only woman he danced with all night. Talk about a double espresso shot to my ego! If we had hashtags back then, I would have been like #BigBitchesRock! I couldn't even fake like I was offended when my sexy Columbus Shortcakes asked if he could go home with me (Note: Columbus Short is a hella fine actor in case you didn't know).

When Being Pretty is a Curse

These incidents of being "chosen" were few and far between until I turned about 26. It was like something happened and the universe opened up and more pretty all over me (or at least that is how people made me feel). In actuality I discovered make-up, high-heels and blonde highlights. I learned how to dress for my body type and exactly what accented my curves and what colors made my cheeks pop. I became fashionable and confident which apparently translated to pretty and sexy, but I had no idea what to do with all that.

I remember going back home for the weekend once with my newly found confidence and fabulous fashion sense in tow. It was always interesting when people that I grew up around came up to me and introduced themselves because they had no idea who I was. It actually got embarrassing when folks that I went to school with would swear they didn't know me until I pulled out old photos.

But the one incident that I remember most vividly is probably because it was the most telling. I had not seen my Great Uncle for nearly 5 years. On a visit back home I convinced my sisters to make the stop by his house. I was excited to see Uncle Chester because he was always so warm and kind to me. When we pulled into the drive way I jumped out of the car and ran on to the porch to ring the doorbell.

My elderly uncle peaked out of the window adjacent to the door and then opened the door slowly. He looked searchingly in my face and said "Can I help you?" I was stunned that he didn't recognize me. I knew he wasn't senile, so I was confused. Before I could speak, my sisters came up behind me and he looked over my shoulder and started to grin. "Heyy girrrls yall come on in" he said in his usual chipper voice. We all filed into his house one by one, each stopping to give him a tight hug as we entered the front room. Once we all sat down, he looked at my oldest sister and point to me "Who dis you got witcha".

I was stunned again, then I blurted out "Uncle Chesterrrrr....It's me J.J.!" He looked at me with narrow eyes then finally a hint of recognition flooded in. "Ohhh my Godddd, J.J. you are soooo beautiful....You're a SWAN." My heart dropped as I asked "well what was I before??" My sister nudged her elbow deep into my arm as Uncle Chester started babbling "you were always errr, cute...but nowwwww well now you are beauuuuuutiful". He tried to cover it up, but he had just unknowingly told me I was an ugly kid that blossomed much later in life. What a damn bummer.

I remember going back to my parents house and pulling out all my school photos and comparing them to my current pictures. I looked the same to me, except for the make-up. But somehow I knew my uncle is right because I had just spent several hours earlier that morning at my home church where I kept hearing "you turned out to be so pretty". And there it was, for the first time in my life, I was the pretty one... there was just one problem. I had no idea what being "pretty" meant.

Over the next few years I became accustomed to being considered pretty. Men gravitated to me and women started to resent me. I could walk into a party and women would instantly plant themselves next to their man to mark their territory. I came to dislike going out with my friends because we would nearly always end up in some skirmish or verbal confrontation because some chick decided she didn't like me. I recall my friend Shannon saying to me once "every time I go somewhere with you, I have to be prepared to fight!".

Then there were the men that followed me out of the grocery store or movie theater to my car to try and get my phone number. And the guys that followed me home or tried to stop me on the freeway. This might have been flattering for many women, but I was mostly nervous and overwhelmed with all the attention. Especially when the men were aggressive.

I had always thought that being pretty would be a blessing, but it started to feel more like a curse. It especially felt like a bad thing when it came to dating. I became something to be pursued and possessed, but not cherished. It's like once I served my purpose to a man, he would discard me and move on. I was simply that thing to be "conquered" and once the victory was complete, they would move on.

I used to think that if a man wanted to sleep with you, it meant that he wanted to be YOUR man". I was naive and trusting, but it hurts to admit that I got used a lot back then. I remember when I really started to resent being the pretty one. I would physically cringe when a man told me I was pretty because in my mind it meant that I was going to be objectified or mistreated before finally being left abandoned and broken hearted. I felt like I needed to be MORE than pretty to truly matter to people, especially men. I mean my "average" friends seemed to stay boo'd up, clearly being pretty was a problem.

I distinctly remember going through a phase when I would ask people NOT to tell me that I was pretty. Most of them would launch into the "you need to learn how to take a compliment" speech. But it wasn't that I couldn't take a compliment, it's that the affirmations were always a precursor to some neglectful or abusive behavior. Especially when the bearer of compliments realized that pretty women will also cut, cuss and fight your ass when you piss us off. My famous line back then was "don't let this pretty face fool ya!"

It would take me years to learn, that my looks would attract all types of people, good and bad. It was up to me to guard and protect myself from the ones who weren't good for me.

An Entire Barrel of Bad Apples

As I stated earlier, I was never considered a "catch" so I didn't have a very high opinion of myself. Not even when my cute score rose and I came to be considered pretty. What other people thought of me, didn't influence me as much of what I thought of myself. Especially considering that I had not been treated very well by the few men that I dated. One of those men in particular turned into what I then considered the love of my life.

I dated Trent (not his real name) off and on for years, but our relationship was never exclusive. He told me at the onset that he wasn't looking for a relationship, and I personally was cool with just dating and hanging out. But nearly I year in, I was head over heels in love with him. All the other men that I had dated found something to nit-pick me apart about. I was always "too ___". Too opinionated, too uptight, too outspoken, too chubby... you name it, I was too much of it. But Trent wasn't like that! He accepted everything about me without complaint or judgment. Or at least non that he verbalized.

When I think back to how grateful I was just to be accepted without criticisms, I get a little emotional. Here I was, damn near 30 and feeling accepted for the first time. But I didn't realize that in this case, there was a caveat to being accepted unconditionally... there actually WERE conditions so to speak. You see Trent openly dated and had sex with other women. He never lied to me or hid that fact from me. I was clear about that when we started dating and my falling in love with him didn't change his behavior.

Somewhere in the back of my mind, I kept thinking that if I was patient enough, eventually he would choose me. I just knew that if I was loving enough and kind enough he would eventually see that I was the greatest love of his life. I remember feeling like we were moving in the right direction when we started to meet each other's family. But nahhh, that commitment never happened. I kept asking myself over and over, "what's wrong with me? Why won't he just chose me?!" We had a number of conversations over the next 2 years about his unwillingness to commit to OUR relationship. And he never told me anything more than he just didn't want a commitment.

He also put me on a 'schedule'. We could see each other only once every other week. On the occasion when I traveled, he might make an exception. But he insisted that he needed a week to himself although I knew that he was seeing other women. From time to time I would get frustrated with this arrangement and blow up at him. This would result in about 2 weeks without seeing each other, but I always went running back to him, because I just couldn't stand to be without him. So ultimately, I agreed to his terms over and over again.

Trent and I were still dating when my Father became paralyzed. He didn't offer much support other than an occasional kind word and a few hugs. Our "schedule" didn't really change though. From time to time, he would come by and give my Dad a haircut on our date night, so then I had to share him with my family.

I can recall a conversation with my sister when I defended Trent's neglectful behavior. I was SUPER angry with her when she told me he wasn't around 80% of the time. I responded "I would rather be alone 80% of the time than 100% of the time" in an angry tone. When I think back on this situation, I weep for that poor girl who was so desperate to be love that she thought that 20% was enough.

I built my entire life around that 20% too. My friends, job, social life were all things I did as distractions while biding my time until I could see Trent again. In terms of a commitment, I was prepared to wait for Trent as long as it took. But in the meantime I started to feel like I simply wasn't good enough. My feelings of inadequacy made me angry, aggressive and bitter. But I was still willing to wait. I loved this man so much, I simply didn't have the strength to walk away. When we finally decided to go our separate ways, it was because he broke up with me through a text message. Now this was like the early 2000's so there were only about 3 folks with text messaging options and we were 2 of them! I'll never forget what that devastating message said "we're done, be out!" Those 4 words shattered my heart into a million pieces and I'm not entirely sure that I have found all the segments yet.

When I say that Trent accepted me unconditionally, I don't think that is quite true. I think his acceptance came with a silent contract for me to accept him with all his bullshit. I blindly signed the contract without reading the fine print. The tiny unspoken statement that said how much damage this situation would cause me. I had no one to translate that this document of unconditional acceptance would leave me with low self worth and high self hate. I was left believing and feeling that I was utterly unlovable.

It took me years to start to date again, 3 years to be exact. I was too broken and wounded to even open myself to finding love again. The truth is, I had not found love the first time... I just fell into a love pit because I wasn't looking where I was going. But eventually I met Trey (I guess I had a thing for men who's names started with TR).

Trey and I certainly spent more time together than I had in my previous relationship. But like Trent, he had no desire to commit to me. And he was very honest that he didn't want to commit to me in particular. I wasn't domestic enough for him. He wanted a woman that was more focused on "wifely" duties than career goals. I remember thinking I could change his mind. I argued my case stating "I could cook for your sometimes, if you want". But he simply responded with "I'm not trying to change you. Just be you..." Bam! Rejected again. I mean this man didn't even want me to waste my time adjusting to his needs when he knew deep down inside, I wasn't what he wanted.

I think what hurt the most is that in the three years we dated he had never told me that I wasn't "the one". It wasn't until I pressured him for more of a commitment that he came clean. He was willing to let me be a bookmark in his life until he was ready to read the next chapter, but I would never be an actual chapter in his book of love.

After Trent and Trey, there was another parade of men that all behaved similarly towards me. And I started to believe that my plight was to be successful, sad and single for life. So what the hell, I might as well enjoy the success part for all it's was worth. I spent most of my 30s focused on creating my success and learning to NOT hate myself.

Doing The Work

Removing self hate is a process. You don't just wake up one day and love yourself. First you have to <u>accept</u> yourself, then <u>like</u> yourself then finally <u>love</u> yourself. Again, it's a process. As I built my business, I also hired a life coach to and we began to do the heavy lifting and put in the work to repair my battered self worth. Let me just be the first to tell you that fixing your sh*t is more than just a notion, it's a lifelong commitment to being your authentically amazing self.

Dr. Imani (my life coach at the time) suggested that start to a journal to encourage the healing process. I found out that writing about my personal struggles was therapeutic, so I began to blog. The first post I wrote wasn't actually a blog, it was written in Facebook Notes (remember those?). The title was **Memoirs of a Fool: How Women's Lib Ruined My Life**. The post went viral with more than 500 comments and thousands of shares around the world.

Going viral back then was a new concept, so I was in shock. I didn't think my perspective was that interesting. I decided that it was a fluke, so I wrote another post, and it also got a lot of traction. Eventually I launched a full blown blog and that drew a sizeable following of readers as well as media outlets. Among them was Essence.com and two years later, I found myself as a regular contributor for them. After about 8 months into my new gig, I penned a blog post that changed the trajectory of my life. The title was **"I Didn't Give Up On Black Men, They Gave Up On Me!"**... I know, the title alone made folks gasp!

As a blogger, I often use my life experiences to explore the theme of self-love. Over the years I've received plenty of positive feedback from women, many of whom told me I made them feel less alone. In the article I explored the challenges I've had dating Black men and lamented that many of them "reject Black women for being too dark, having short hair or being plus size."

Within hours of the piece going up, the insults began. "You could stand to lose a few pounds," posted someone who called herself Lola. "Looking at your picture, can you blame them?" added Kayla. When links to my story appeared on The Root and MadameNoire, things really got out of hand. "Every fat woman I've ever known lived in denial, just like you," blasted Quiet Thoughts II. Readers Googled images of me and posted the pictures in comment threads so that everyone could chime in on how "obese" or "undesirable" they thought I was.

At first I tried to respond to the comments, but it was all too much. These readers were tagging my Facebook fan page, insulting me on Twitter, and posting one hateful jab after another. Someone even created a YouTube video dedicated to ridiculing me. The article went up on a Thursday, and by Saturday I had shut down all my social media accounts. Even that wasn't enough to avoid the nasty comments. When I logged on to my computer to check e-mail, I was horrified to find that people had sought out my personal Web site and used it to send more angry comments. This was supposed to be a happy moment in my career—the article was my most viewed ever on ESSENCE.com—but it hardly mattered. I told myself I had been stupid to share such a personal story and wondered if maybe the hecklers were right. Maybe fat people do belong in the shadows; at least there I would feel safe.

I spent the weekend in bed with my head under the covers balling my brown eyes out. I also strategized the over the entire weekend of exactly how I could quit Essence without making a big stink. I called my editor Monday, to deliver the news. To this day I have to say how thankful I am for Charli, she listened and supported me and then shared some sage advice. She told me about her own experiences and then she said something that changed my life. "Jai, if they are coming for you like this, it means you have arrived. All the top bloggers go through this, this how they stay relevant." she explained. Wait, what?! Did she mean this bullsh*t was normal?

My confirmation came a week later as I watched Oprah Winfrey's Super Soul Sunday on OWN. Best-selling author Brené Brown recounted a negative experience she had after her TED talk on vulnerability went viral. Viewers insulted her appearance all over the Web. I discovered that when it came to online bullying, I was hardly alone. Technology, with the access and anonymity it allows, breeds this kind of meanness. It wasn't a coincidence that the most vicious comments came from people using fake names and generic avatars.

Meeting Bishop T.D. Jakes

Charli (my editor) had suggested that I write through the pain. Six weeks later I penned a follow-up blog post called "Why Is She So Fat?" in which I addressed the comments about my weight and explained that I learned long ago not to judge my worth by the numbers on a scale. I was sending a message that I would not be bullied into silence or shamed into going away. I stood up for myself, and for the first time in weeks, I felt good again.

A few days after the piece was posted, a TV producer from BET called and said that she had read my article and she loved it! She then invited me be the featured guest on T.D. Jakes's new talk show.

About 2 months later, I found myself sitting in my driveway with my sister in the back of a black SUV. BET had sent a car service to bring me to the studio for a filming my show. When I arrived, there were producers and staff lined the hall to greet me and introduce themselves. They told me what role they had in filming my introductory video (shot the week before) or how they would play a role in the production that day.

I was ushered to my own dressing room that had a sitting area in it. My sister Rhonda and Lifestyle Coach Akilah joined me to help calm my nerves. The producers helped choose my outfit and then I was bombarded by the glam squad. The team that did my hair and makeup were custom selected because they had also worked on Monique's show and they understood how to make a curvy girl sparkle on camera. Susan and Marilyn (two producers) also came into the room to make sure I didn't need any more special arrangements. What can I say, I felt like a Hollywood starlet!

When I was all ready, they ushered me out onto the set. I sat down and I could see Rhonda and Akilah in the audience. I also caught a glimpse of several more of my friends who had managed to get tickets to the taping. And then it happened, the theater lights when down and the stage lights came on and Bishop T.D. Jakes himself walked out on stage. He briefly addressed the audience then my demo reel started. When the clip finished and the stage lights came back on, I could see a few audience members wiping away tears.

Then Bishop walked across the stage in long deliberate strides that allowed him to cover the distance in just a few short steps. He sat on the seat next to me and then started a conversation. There was no script, I didn't know the questions in advance. I had no choice but to be present, be open and be honest.

At some point he said to me "I was reading your file" (insert T.D. Jakes voice here). I know he said something after that, but I swear I have do cotton picking idea what he said. All I kept thinking in my head is "a sista got a file with TD JAKES!!!". And in case you are wondering, he is every bit as profound and amazing in person as he is on television. To be honest with you, before that day I had just seen him as a greatly profound orator, but that day I came to understand that he was also divinely anointed.

Later that summer, my episode of the show aired and was viewed by more than a million households around the world. I got emails, tweets and messages from people around the world. I couldn't help but to think, that as devastating as the cyber-bullying had been, standing up to the bullies opened the door to the experience of a lifetime.

I had finally learned not to let other people determine my worth based on my appearance or judge whether I deserve to be loved. Because the REAL truth is, until you know my journey, you're not qualified to judge me!

As I take stock of the person that I am today. I can say that for the first time since I can remember, I truly love the person that I am. I live my life without fear or apologies for my flaws or imperfections. And while I'm not actually a celebrity, I can say I felt like one on that day when I sat at the feet of Bishop T. D. Jakes and he spoke over my life.

So the next time I overhear someone ask, why is she so fat? I will think to myself, who cares... she's simply fabulous!

Conversations with My Children

FELICIA PHILLIPS

. . . .

I will always protect you," were my last words to my daughter before she went to bed that night. I kissed her, and my baby boy, then laid next to them waiting for them to go to sleep. They looked so innocent as the moonlight shined across their faces. I let out a long breath and then took in a deep one. I knew exactly what was about to happen, but I needed to be cool. I didn't want to seem anxious or nervous. Once I knew they were out for the count, I slipped out of the bed and left the door cracked.

I walked down the hall pretending like I was finishing my last little bit of cleaning and then going to bed too. My husband was already in the master suite, "Felicia!" he called out to me. "What are you doing and why aren't you in bed yet?" I stopped in my tracks and took another deep breath; he would not ruin my plan. He always wanted to control every part of the situation, especially when it involved me. "I'm coming!" I replied.

I entered the room and looked in his direction avoiding any eye contact. I decided to take a long, hot shower replaying every part of my plan in my head. When I felt confident, I exited and prepared myself as usual. I could feel him watching me and tonight I was going to take my sweet time. This was it and I was ready. The plan was in motion.

What have I done? Lord! What have I done? I thought, full of fear and driving aimlessly, speeding to nowhere or at least that's what I thought. The roads were dark and visibility was low, but I didn't care. We're free! I shouted to myself, as my children who were ages two and five lay sleeping in their car seats without a wrinkle in their brow. I needed to reassure myself that what I did was right. I told myself this move is what's best for us, as the night engulfed our car, I felt certain in my decision. Then I found myself not just laughing but, crying with joy. I did it! You see, after six years I finally got the courage to leave him, leave my husband. Let me take you back a few years.

After eight years, he was no longer the man I fell in love with and had become the man I despised. I hated him. I felt like he had taken away everything I loved about myself and I lost my identity. Gradually over the course of the years we had been together, he had separated me from my friends and people I cared about. His friends replaced my friends. I wanted my marriage to work, but I couldn't take any more abuse from him and especially not in front of my children.

My poor babies were suffering too. I could see the fear in their eyes every time our voices would raise as insults began to hurl through the air. Shoving, shouting, screaming, cursing...how had it come to this? Obviously, I missed all the signs when we were dating. This craziness became our daily routine. Every time, he slammed a door, got in my face, degraded me, and even threatened me, I knew I was losing a part of who I was inside.

I was becoming angrier with each passing day. That could not be good for our children. I was fed up with not only the abuse, but the lies, the deceit, not to mention the infidelity. I was so stressed out, it was all just too much for me to handle. Then he started withdrawing large sums of money from our checking account and could not legitimately explain what happened to it. He was out of control all the way around, and from my vantage point we were at the point of no return.

Around the second year of our marriage, I started having migraines dealing with the intensity of it all and little did I know at the time, I was pregnant with our second child. I felt like I was losing my sense of reality. I remember scheduling an appointment once I realized I was pregnant. When I arrived for my appointment, I sat in the waiting room feeling nervous. I knew our marriage was on the rocks and being pregnant did not help the situation between us, nor did I feel it would change things for the better.

I wasn't naïve enough to believe that the birth of this beautiful child would reverse the damage that had already been done. They called my name and escorted me to the examining room to wait for my physician. During my examination, the doctor told me my blood pressure and stress levels were extremely high. "Go figure," I said to myself.

They sent me home with a special diet that they thought would do the trick. A week to the day of my visit, I was feeling really bad. My head was pounding and my vision was blurry, I felt like I was going to throw-up from the nausea and dizziness. I recall dropping my daughter at daycare and then going to the office. On my way there, I began to see spots and lines across my eyes, which made it hard for me to drive. The back of my head was pounding. I pulled into the parking lot, then everything after that faded to black.

When I came to my good friend was standing next to me crying. She told me she found me in the elevator on the floor. She didn't even wait for an ambulance. She rushed me straight to the hospital. I went to sit up and I immediately knew something was grossly wrong. I could barely move. My parents were in the room as well, I could see the tears in my father's eyes and the fear in my mother's.

My father laid his hand gently on my chest to motion to me to relax and lay back down. When I tried to talk, I couldn't. Wait, I could not talk! The next thing I noticed was that my husband was not in the room. I could see my reflection, my face didn't look right to me, I had a slight shift as if the right sight had shifted downward. I closed my eyes and thought, "Why me God?"

It was so surreal, I asked myself why was that happening to me and being concerned about my baby. Was my baby going to be alright? I felt awful, I was frightened about my future. I cried, silently, on the inside. My whole body hurt. The doctor told me they couldn't treat me for the stroke the way they normally did because I was pregnant, but they would do the best they could nevertheless.

What in the hell did that mean? I just wanted the doctor to say that my baby and I were going to be ok. Hours later, my husband showed up! I felt angry, what took him so long? How dare he just cruise into the room and he didn't even look concerned.

He said to me, "I wasn't sure what you would look like, I'm stressed too." Really? If I could have punched him in his mouth, I would have. No concern, no love, no consideration. He didn't even ask if our baby was alright. That was unbelievable. I saw the sheer anger and frustration in my parents' eyes. I felt humiliated and disgusted. I had been diagnosed by the neurologist as having suffered a light stroke and was released a few days later.

After returning home on bed rest, I was assigned physical therapy a couple times a week. Although my husband and I were in the same house, we were not together. We were strangers passing each other in the wind. Our conversation had no depth, our love had no meaning. My mother loved and supported me for seven months, caring and nurturing until I gave birth to a beautiful 10 pound baby boy.

He looked so peaceful when they laid him across my chest. Holding him in my arms, I felt renewed. He gave me the strength I needed to pull myself back together. With all that was going on, the chaos and my struggling marriage, a new life had entered into the scenario. He definitely did not deserve that type of confusion. I prayed for direction, and knowing that my situation was bleak, I left the hospital with hope that something would change soon.

However, that was wishful thinking, nothing changed just more of the same. Now my husband was staying out more and was beginning to act really weird about his whereabouts. When I asked him about where he had been and why he was coming home so late he told me, "You, just worry about the kids, I got this." I wasn't that out of my mind. I suspected he was having an affair, but the way I found out was humiliating.

One evening, I was home playing with the children when the phone rang. It was an old friend of mine, I was glad to hear from her. After we exchanged pleasantries, she said, "Felicia, I am calling for a different reason tonight." She began to tell me how she was out with some friends and saw my husband in my car with another woman. At first glance she thought it was me, but when she reached the car she could clearly see not only that it was not me, but that he was kissing another woman.

I couldn't say a word. For some reason, it was different for me as long as no one knew about the abuse and the things I was tolerating. Hearing about his infidelity frm somebody else made me want to explode. That was definitely the last straw and in my gut I knew it was true. She described him down to the shoes he had on that day.

Unbelievable! I managed to get enough words out to thank her and then I spent the rest of the evening putting my plan in together. It was time to leave. I had no words for him, I was fed up. I was not going to shame myself in front of my children by getting into an argument with him, when I already knew the truth. My plan to leave was in motion. The funny thing was, as bad as I wanted to leave, I didn't have the courage right away. I didn't realize what the years had done to my psyche.

Every time I would get ready to walk out the door, something held me back...fear. So for two years I consumed myself in the business and my children, until courage found me.

* * *

Here I was a couple years later on a dark road in the middle of the night with a made up mind to take back control over my life. I was done and I was not going to take that kind of treatment anymore. Leaving, especially stealing away in the middle of the night, was a hard thing to do after building so much together. So much!

When we married we had a plan to conquer the world. We were both smart entrepreneurs and we looked good together. I thought to myself, we are blessed to have one another. Although he had been married before and he was almost 20 years my senior, I believed we were the perfect match. You couldn't tell me that man wasn't my soul mate. He made me feel special, as if I was the only person who mattered to him. I was young and eager to make my mark on this world.

I was nineteen when we meet, he was thirty-six, we dated for four years and then married. He did it all, expensive dates, flowers all the time, shopping sprees, extravagant vacations and he even listened to my dreams and helped me in my business. Six years later, we had several successful businesses, money, cars, a beautiful home on three acres and a marriage that was killing me slowly everyday.

One morning, I walked into the master bathroom and glimpsed myself walking past the mirror. I barely recognized myself. The stress had taken a toll on me. I caressed my face gently, I looked much older than twenty-eight. I looked tired. Funny, my great grandmother would jokingly say, "An old man will steal your youth." Maybe she was right, because what I saw in the mirror was definitely a reflection of her statement.

Almost six months after being married, my husband began to dictate my every move. He told me what I should listen to, who we socialized with, what to read and even how I should dress. I felt like he was suffocating me. I didn't like that feeling at all. Four years later, after the birth of my babies, he began to tell me over and over how no man would ever want me. He said, I had too much baggage. I was no good to any man after having two babies and a light stroke. He laughed and said, "Who would want you?" He went on to tell me that I should be glad that he still loved and cared me. Every day I lost a piece of myself. I felt empty inside, I was so unhappy.

I worked tirelessly in our business day and night to avoid his abusive tirades. My work had paid off in a big way for us. We had multiple business locations and were grossing seven figures easy. Even with all that success, we couldn't find our happy place together. We were moving in two very different directions. The years of chaos had not only worn me down, it had even taken a toll on my daughter.

Every time my husband and I fought, she would take her baby brother in her room and lock the door until I came to retrieve them. She was scared. I remember her telling me, "Mommy, I'd rather live in a hotel room, than to live in this house." She was only five years old! I froze when she said those words. That afternoon I looked at her and made a promise that I would always keep her and her brother safe. They were everything to me and I would not raise them in a home they weren't comfortable in. The whole situation was unimaginable, but yet it was my reality.

The promise to keep them safe haunted me all day. I couldn't sleep, I could almost see my heart beating in my chest, I was beyond scared. My mind was racing, I turned over and the clock read 3:47 a.m. I eased out of the bed, put their car seats in the car and with calculated steps, went to get my babies. They looked so peaceful in their beds. I knew once I picked them up, their lives would be forever changed. I took a deep breath and moved swiftly, my mind was made up, the right moment for me to leave had come.

As I drove, full of emotions and thoughts racing through my head, I looked up and found myself at my parent's home. This was the last place I wanted to be because I did not want to put my loved ones in harm's way. The truth is, I couldn't think of anywhere else to go with my babies and I was a mess. As my finger touched the door bell, I broke down again. Weeping I fell into my father's arms, he never asked one question, his reply was simply, "What do you need me to do?"

He helped me get the kids out of the car and put them to bed. I sat in the room on the bed where they were sleeping and began to pray. I was so scared of what my husband might do, yet I knew God had my back. I was afraid he might come looking for us, possibly getting really violent. I didn't want my parents in harm's way. My mind kept racing. This would not be my forever. I went downstairs to the kitchen for a cup of tea and went for a walk to clear my head. I needed to get a strategy in place for me and the kids.

I finally laid down and rested, knowing there was so much that had to be done before I could be at ease. I wanted my marriage to be over so badly that I actually filed the paperwork myself. The very next day, I went to Office Depot, got the template and prepared it myself.

Days later as I walked into the courthouse, I felt no hesitancy, no regret I knew I had done everything within my power to save my marriage. The clerk told me this would be a 30 day process and I was elated to hear those words. Finally, 30 days later I was in courtroom and the Judge noticed I'd asked for nothing in the divorce decree.

He chuckled and said, "Ma'am. I cannot let you leave here with nothing." He ordered my soon to be ex-husband to pay child support. Don't get too excited, it was only $400 a month and I knew in my heart he wouldn't pay it. We left the courthouse, my now ex-husband said, "I hope you wind up in a homeless shelter." His words only fueled my desire to succeed.

The kids and I moved into an apartment a couple days later. I made a decision to leave everything, all my possessions in the marital home and walk away with nothing. I needed peace of mind more than anything material. He told our friends and family that I'd lost my mind...gone crazy. He even said he had no idea why I left him.

We went into that apartment with only a bed, which I was grateful to have. The reality was, I had never felt so happy. It was a new beginning for the children and I. After being on my own since I was 17 years old, I was now faced with starting from scratch. I had to reassess my financial situation and put a plan in place. I had to know how we would survive.

I awoke early the next morning. The kids laid in the bed with me sleeping soundly. I began to make a list of what needed to be done next. I drove to Carmax, I had to make some immediate moves to get us back on track financially. The last thing I wanted was for my babies to suffer or go without. I was not going to ask for handouts, because, this was my situation and in all honestly I needed to know that I could take care of us.

When the salesman walked towards me, I felt my heart beating so fast it hurt. I placed the keys in his hand and told him I wanted to sell my car and buy another. Hours later I was signing papers selling the convertible Red Lexus SC430 with cream leather seats, and we left in a used green Mercury Mystique with grey cloth interior. Every move I made was a step down. And it felt like a punch in the gut, yet those moves were in the right direction.

My daughter had a confused look on her face when they drove the car around. When we got in the car, my daughter asked me, "Mommy are we poor?" I felt sick to my stomach. Her words stung like an angry wasp, I wanted to kick, scream and cry. The one thing I trusted with all my heart is what my great-grandmother told me as a child, "God will not put more on you than your can bear." I was trusting God to give me the insight and wisdom I needed to get through this situation.

I looked at my daughter who was anxiously awaiting an answer from her Mother. I saw the innocence and trust in her eyes. I began to explain as best I could to a child that life had drastically changed for us. Believe it or not I had a real, down to earth conversation about where we were financially in a way that a child could understand. I did not hide the fact that things would be rough for us initially, but what I asked her was to trust Mommy. Trust that we would not be in this position long. Trust that Mommy made this decision hoping for a better life. I finished by reinforcing that I loved her and her brother with every fiber of my being. I would let nothing stop us from being a family.

She looked at me and said, "I know Mommy, it's like you always say we are a team. I love you." Yes! Yes! Yes! We were a team. Thank you God, her words meant everything to me.

I am a believer that you have to constantly communicate with your children. I would never talk to them like they were babies, nor would I talk to them like they were adults. While I wanted them to remain in a child-like state, while knowing I had their back every step of the way. Just hearing her say those words made me stronger. In that moment, I felt revived.

I repositioned myself and started another my business. I enrolled them in a new school and when school was over

I took them to work with me. They stayed in the conference room while I worked at my desk. I would put them in the conference room with food, movies and even their homework, checking on them between calls and appointments with clients. A surveillance camera in the room allowed me to watch them.

It's funny how everyone could give me their two cents about raising my children, but no one really wanted to help. That didn't stop me. More people thought I was wrong than right, but I did what I had to do to take care of my family. I was focused and on a mission to take my life back. I did what I had to do every day because I promised my children that we would have a better life.

I had many conversations about our "type" of family, where it was just me and them. I told them because we were a team we could accomplish anything and deep down I meant it. Every word of it. I intended on keeping my promise for us to build a life beyond what we once knew. After 15 months of sacrificing, saving and building my business, we were in our new home and life was good.

They were finally getting settled back into a stable environment. My divorce was finalized, I had put my past behind me, but there was still something and someone I was dealing with, my son. The entire time I was struggling to bring some normalcy to our lives, I was dealing with the diagnosis of my son being autistic.

He was four years old and still he wasn't speaking. It was if he had slipped into a world of darkness. The most difficult part was shielding him from thoughtless and cruel people who talked as if he were not in listening range. Asking questions in front of him saying things like, "What's wrong with him?" "Why does he make those sounds?" "Why can't he speak?"

I wanted to hold him and keep him from the cruelty of this world, but I knew that couldn't happen. So I fought for him, I would not give up on him. I studied autism, asked questions, took classes and continuously worked with him. I began to see some progress, but we still had a long ways to go. Later, I found out he was being mistreated and neglected at school. My daughter came home and explained that she had seen him in his classroom sitting at a table by himself on several occasions all alone.

I decided to show up at the school unannounced and sure enough there he was sitting by himself. I was furious. How could they do such a thing? They were teachers! Didn't they take an oath? Didn't they care? I wasn't naïve, I knew my son had challenges. However, I didn't expect this. I withdrew them both from the school after meeting with their staff and realizing that was not the place for my children. I had to save my son by changing yet again.

Taking time away from my business and learning everything I could in order to help him, I asked my mother for her help. She had teaching experience and was excellent at working with children. She was right there with me every step of the way. We worked together to defeat the odds, to give my son a fighting chance. I was determined not to let him be labeled and not to let him be a statistic. I took him to be tested again and found it was Asperger's, a form of autism.

Armed with the proper information, I began to make some immediate changes. I changed his diet to mostly organic and began to give him Omega-3. I did more exercises to strengthen the left side of his brain. I detoxed our entire home after finding out our home was affecting him as well. Out went all the chemicals; bleach, toxic cleaners, aerosols and I even changed the detergent I washed his clothes in too. This change was good for us all.

Making changes wasn't comfortable, but I saw such wonderful progress. I was happy for him, I could see the light returning. Something else was happening, I was changing too. My prayer life increased three fold. I was believing God for a miracle in my son. I would go in his room at night and pray over him. When he woke up, I would always say to him, "Son, I know God is going to do something great with you today, you are a blessed child." I began to repeat God's promises back to Him.

I was giving all I had, I was not going to give up on him. I was determined free my son from the darkness that had taken over his life. There were moments at night when the kids would be asleep that I would just lay across my bed looking at the ceiling, tears running down the side of my face, repeating to myself over and over, "I can do this." We had been through so much together. I just wanted them to be kids. I wanted them not to have a care in the world. I was their mother, this was my duty to them and I was going to fulfill it.

●　●　●

Finally, I found a school that I felt would support his needs. I met with every teacher that had to work with him during the day, as well as the principal. I researched every program and resource that was available to him. The teachers were awesome. They went above and beyond to make him feel comfortable and it was beginning to pay off. He began participating in class and playing with other children. I know that may sound like nothing much, but for him this was huge and I couldn't have been happier about it.

I remember one day in particular, after years of me speaking words of affirmation into him, he walked in the door from school, shut the door and called out to me. My eyes, got so big and my heart began to beat, this was not normal behavior. He hardly spoke at all. He looked me in the eye and a big smile came over his face and then he said, "Mom, I'm smart!" I felt my chest explode and my eyes began to water as I fought to hold back the tears. All I could say was, "Yes son, you are smart!"

I was completely overwhelmed with the goodness of God. I was grateful for our days ahead. It seemed as if the sun was shining on us and it felt warm. After years of pushing, praying and positioning us for a better life, we had it. It was three years later and the business I started with no money and leaving my children in the boardroom while I worked was now a multi-million dollar business with multiple locations.

Life was finally looking up for us and I was grateful. Did I just say that? Wow! My business was now grossing over a million a year. I did it with no money, but a lot of sweat equity and hard work.

All the sacrifice, sleepless nights, tears and bouts of depression and anger were paying off. I built a multi-million dollar real estate finance company and was in the process of expanding. "God is faithful," I said silently to myself. My mother and I continued to work with my son. Eventually, my son was able to overcome his battle with autism and went on to maintain honor roll from third grade to the present and he was inducted into the National Beta Club.

I remember watching him during the induction ceremony. Thinking of all the things the teachers and other professionals said about him in our meetings. They told me his future was anything but promising. Looking at him now, I am proud. My daughter, who many felt I kept it too real with, has now graduated from high school and moving on to fulfilling her passion in the beauty industry. She is happy about her life and she has grown into a beautiful, caring woman. I am thankful for my new level of peace. Just when I believed it could not get any better, something amazing happened. I found love again after almost 10 years of being divorced.

I reconnected with a former friend and classmate through, Facebook of all things. We talked offline for months before even going on our first date. I really enjoyed his conversations. He was recently divorced and oh boy was he handsome. Initially, I thought it would be nice to just to date, to have a romantic interest. Six months later, we finally went out on our first date.

It was everything I'd hoped for and much more. He was a wonderful gentleman. Can you believe we went on a date almost every night that first week? It was so wonderful, better than I could have ever expected. One day, after a month and a half of dating, we were having lunch and he said he had something on his heart he wanted to share with me. His words were, "I don't want to just date you, I want you to be my wife."

I gasped, the biggest smile spread across my face. Did he just say that? It was like music to ears, a song to my heart. I jokingly said, "Are you asking me to marry you?" Ninety days after our first date, we were married. The intimate ceremony was perfect with close friends and family. The best part of it all was that the kids were just as happy as I was about having a new member to "our type" of family. Our wedding was perfect.

You never know the direction life will take you. After all, I had almost become use to the chaos and there always being some sort of stress for me to deal with but, times had changed and that was alright with me. I really found out through my trials and tribulations who I was and what I was made of.

So many negative things had happened in my past I almost believed it was a way of life for me. That wasn't true, but it had been my experience for years. I welcomed this new chapter of my life. I had to release my past or it would damage everything I'd worked to build. Changing your mindset is a daily process when so many things have occurred in your life to destroy you. The thing I had to realize is that each incident only made me stronger. My journey was not just for me, but for other women who may be experiencing the same things. For years I kept my story locked inside, but now I'm releasing it! My only hope is that it empowers others.

Divorced & Down, but Not Dead

MEOCHIA CLAYTON

• •

N ovember 20, 1995 will be a day that I will never forget, it's the day my son was born. The circumstances were far from typical. It's been approximately 20 years, but I still remember that day as if it were yesterday. I was nine months pregnant and was scheduled for an 11:00 a.m. weekly prenatal visit. I was explaining to my obstetrician how fetal movement had decreased over the past couple of days and I was wondering whether that was normal since I was at the end of the pregnancy. My doctor immediately sent me for a sonogram and confirmed that complications had developed. My baby had detached from the placenta and they would have to perform an emergency caesarian section. I called my husband and told him that he would have to come to the hospital as soon as possible because the baby was coming that day.

While I was hooked up to all of the hospital equipment, the nurse would ask me from time to time, "Did you feel that?" I would state no and she would tell me each time that I had just had a contraction. I didn't feel anything, I only remember having all of these thoughts and feeling alone since there was no one there to talk to.

This is the child that my family members and friends felt was long overdue. I had been married to my husband for five years and everyone felt that we should have already started a family a within that time. Over the years, I heard so many reasons why we should start a family. "You are almost 30 years old and you need to start soon." "If you are afraid that you can't afford a child, just look around you, the Lord isn't going to have you birth a child that He won't provide for." "You are married, what's the problem?"

The one statement that really sticks out in my mind is when my grandmother said, "I wish you or your sister would have a baby before I die." Her words alone had more influence on my decision to start a family than any of the others that I received throughout the years. I loved and admired my grandmother with all I have in me. For her to have raised nine children and loved them each unconditionally, I wanted to experience that same type of love.

As I waited for my husband to arrive at the hospital, I prayed and prayed. I felt that time was of the essence and everyone seemed to be taking theirs. Things couldn't move as fast as I wanted them to. That day had to be the longest day ever. Once my husband arrived, the medical staff prepped me for the emergency procedure. I was given an epidural and was warned prior to administering that the needle would be very painful; however, I needed to stay as still as possible. I really didn't feel any pain at all.

The events of that day were surreal, it was if I knew everything that was going on around me, but I felt numbness. If I had to sum the events of that day, it was like an out of body experience. I was so focused on birthing this baby into this world, the doctors could have done anything they wanted to me and I would have endured it. My husband told me that the needle was long, and he asked me how you could not feel that. I had no words, I was just purposely waiting for our baby to be delivered.

Once in the delivery room, they draped me so I wouldn't see the actual procedure. Our baby was born at 8:00 p.m. I was waiting to hear a cry, some sort of sign that there was life and there was nothing! Immediately after he was taken from my body, they rushed him to the Neonatal Intensive Care Unit, or NICU. I told my husband to follow them because our baby needed him more than I did at that time. Once again I was alone with my thoughts and my fears now to wonder and worry about what's going on with my baby.

Once I was stitched up, they sent me to the recovery room and later released to my own room. That night became the longest night ever and I was so alert. Every time the door to my hospital room opened, I just knew they were coming to tell me that my son did not make it. My husband came to my room to tell me that our baby had several seizures while in the NICU and that he was really big. That information helped and it didn't help. I really needed a doctor to come and tell me what was going on. The fear of the unknown had me in a very uncomfortable place, I couldn't sleep and I didn't want to eat until somebody could give me some information as to what was really going on with my baby.

Finally, the neonatal doctor came to my room and told me that my baby was fighting, he had three seizures and he was not breathing on his own. He said that the baby was placed in a state as if he was still in my womb. I felt perplexed, how could this be? This is the child that I nurtured in my womb for nine months. I did everything that I was told to do by my doctors, as well as from books that I had read. Could I have done more?

They put him in a medically induced coma state since what he went through in my womb was similar to trauma that someone would go through as a result of a head injury. I was informed that he was born asphyxiated, he was not breathing at the time of his birth and he had to be stabilized and placed on a ventilator. The doctor asked me whether I knew my son's weight and I told him I didn't. He stated that he was 10 pounds and 4 ounces. I could only say WOW, which basically confirmed what I felt in my heart. I felt that my predicted delivery date was incorrect, my son was overdue. I felt he should have been born at least two weeks prior. I questioned whether I could have been more persistent about the date I felt he should have been due.

It was after midnight, when the nurse wheeled me to the neonatal unit to see my baby. I laid eyes on my beautiful child in an incubator with tubes everywhere and his eyes were closed, he was in a very deep sleep. I held his precious, tiny hand and touched his fingers. There is just something missing for a new mother when you can't hear your child's first cry and you can't hold them in your arms. It's just something incomplete in the birthing process when these two things don't happen. I asked the doctors and nurses many questions about my child's condition, but I refused to ask them whether he was going to survive. That conversation was between me and God, I didn't think a human alive could give me that answer and furthermore, I wasn't going to give them a chance to answer that question.

I stayed in the hospital for three days and not much had changed in my son's condition. Well, that was my perspective since he wasn't crying, his eyes weren't open, and he wasn't acting like a newborn. However, the nurses would continuously tell me that his vital signs were good and that he was doing so well. God bless all those neonatal nurses, I don't know what I would have done without their positive demeanor. They gave me hope and I trusted them since they saw babies in different conditions on a daily basis.

On one occasion, while visiting my son, the neonatologist that cared for him immediately after his birth was there checking my son's vitals. He looked at me and he said, I have been off for the past three days and I was not expecting to see your son here when I returned. He told me that my son had started to go through the process of dying, his tissues were starting to die when he was delivered.

He continued to say that he really didn't think that my son would make it and because he is still here he must have some type of purpose. I could see the confusion on his face, he just didn't know what to think. He left me with these words, "He has gone through a lot, watch him because he may experience problems later on in his development. When it's time, take him home and enjoy him." Hearing that made me feel hopeful and guarded at the same time. As any other parent, I didn't know how things would turn out. I just knew that I would be there for my son.

* • ⊚ ⊛

Well, the staff couldn't keep me in the hospital. I was told that my insurance company would not allow me to stay because, I was well and ready to go home. My doctor said, "I am trying to find something wrong with you...a fever, anything...since you are healthy, you have to be discharged. I really wanted to stay there with my baby, it was so hard for me to leave him there.

The separation made me feel sad and I left carrying the burden that I was leaving a part of me behind. Unfortunately, I had no other choice, I had to go home, but I made sure that I was visited him every day. My family and friends would make a fuss because I had just gone through a C-section. They yelled about me needing time to heal then joking that the baby would be home soon enough and I won't be able to get any rest then. I didn't and couldn't listen to them, I was never in any pain from the surgery. I never took the Percocet and or the other medication that was prescribed, I was fine.

I had to be there for my child to make sure that he would be fine. Each morning, I went to the hospital and every evening I left crying. One day, a neonatal nurse asked me, "Why are you crying?" I didn't have an answer for her, I just couldn't stop crying. She said, "He's doing fine and he's going to be just fine!" That I came in the hospital and my son's eyes were open and he was looking around brought me indescribable joy. There was life in my child and that was the moment I felt that he was going to be alright.

Three weeks later, my son was released to go home. That was a very happy day for me and my husband. My family and friends were right, I didn't get much rest after he was discharged. He cried all the time, it was as if he was in pain because he didn't like to be handled. The doctors couldn't explain other than to say there are some babies who don't like to be touched. Within two months time, he got used to being held, carried and soon began to react to us and many objects that newborns notice, such as ceiling fans.

I started to notice every little detail of his development and would refer to the book *What to Expect the First Year*, and prepared a list of notes to provide his doctor on each visit. In many ways, being a mother came naturally for me, so I didn't have any problems caring for my child. It was my marriage that began to change, things were different.

The dynamics of the marriage began to change. Instead of my husband and I being one, my husband saw my son and I as one. I say that because if my husband wasn't speaking to me or upset with me, he would also ignore our son. I could never understand that, even today

I am still confused by those actions. I had to be there for my newborn child and I know that set the stage of events that caused problems in my marriage. I don't know for certain whether the relationship was weak in the beginning, but I knew we were starting to experience the beginning of the end of the marriage.

Growing up around a lot of strong women caused me to be very strong when it came to survival and, taking care of myself, however it made me ill-prepared in relating to men. I didn't have male role models in my life to show and tell me how I was to be treated as a woman, as wife, and as a mother. So early in the marriage I took a lot of things I probably should not have, and by that point, I felt I deserved better. I do know that what I endured with my child changed me forever. I was no longer fearful of my husband leaving, because I was no longer the Meochia he married. I began to see a shift in my life and God was shaping me to be the person He purposed me to be.

I was there for my son 100 percent. I had to be! I was his mother and every fiber of his being needed to be protected. He started to reach all of his developmental milestones along with his peers. He turned over, sat up, crawled, and walked as expected by his pediatrician. He even started to speak in complete sentences.

It was at the age of 3, when I noticed that he stopped building his vocabulary skills and he actually started to regress in his development. The words and sentences that he was consistently using started to decrease and it eventually got to the point where he had lost all of his speech. He no longer had any words. Mama...Daddy...all of his words were gone. The words that his newborn neonatologist came flooding back to me, "Watch him because he may have problems later in his development".

My son started school at three years old in an early learning program to identify any learning disabilities and to provide early intervention. Navigating the special education process is an experience within itself. There were numerous Individualized Education Program (IEP) meetings, in attempt to find out what my child needed to progress, which really became a daunting task year after year. I knew something was wrong. Going through the waiting without having anything concrete to stand on made me fearful on what the future would bring.

Initially, he was diagnosed with developmental delay, which I later found out was the first label given since educational professionals avoid making a firm diagnosis at an early age. The diagnosis of autism came around the age of six, due to my son's cognitive and verbal skills remaining severely delayed. That was confirmation of what my heart felt all along.

The years passed, and a lot of time and focus had to go into the care of my son. Many of the things that his peers were able to do independently, such as dress themselves and care for their basic needs, I had to do for my son. During those years, my marriage was still very fragile and when my son turned six, I realized that my marriage was irretrievably broken. Eventually, we both came to that conclusion and we decided to divorce. We basically lived separate lives and mentally, I think we had both left the marriage. There wasn't one particular event that caused me to feel that way, it was a culmination of feelings. We deserted each other and became less important to each other. We had problems in the past, from our courtship to the time that we got married, and before we had our child, I was so afraid of him leaving me.

At that time, I made the decision to take the forefront in caring for our child and make sure that he has the best life possible. I was going to be a single parent and I made a choice not to be angry because it would not help our situation. I agree that there were times in the marriage where I allowed the focus on my child to take precedent over the relationship with my husband.

He would say things such as, "You may not be the best at a lot of things, but you are a good mother to our child." I took that statement in offense because I thought he was comparing all my shortcomings to me being a mother. I could have very well have turned things around and said the same about him. It made me upset that he had higher standards for me as a mother than he held for himself as our child's father.

Honestly, I didn't feel that I had a choice, based on how I was raised I felt the child came first, and the child that God had blessed me with has caused me to take an unconventional approach. I did what I felt was best at that time and what I felt I could live with.

I was raised primarily by women, my mother, my grandmother, and my aunts. My grandmother was the matriarch and she was a very strong lady. She proudly raised nine children alone and she had no problems telling anyone that she would put her children over any man. I grew up hearing her say that her children were all that she had and they came first in her life after God.

She taught all of her female children, grandchildren, and great-grandchildren that it was possible to be strong and independent women. Not only did she teach this, she demonstrated it for many years. As far as I'm concerned, she wore an invisible "S" on her chest and I know that I carry a piece of her around with me. She gave us no other choice but to be strong.

I remember when I was about eleven years old, she was teaching me how to fry chicken when I got the worst steam burn on my hand. I didn't know that steam could cause that much pain. I told my grandmother about the pain thinking she was going to tell me that she would take over. Surprisingly, she told me to run cold water over my hand and finish cooking that chicken. That was the type of woman she was, she didn't give you the option to give up. You did what you had to do to keep on moving forward.

When my marriage ended, it hurt, but I knew that I had to be there for my son. I felt abandoned and upset with him that he had a choice to whether he wanted to be an active parent. He had a decision as to whether he wanted to see him every other weekend and holidays. For me, that was not a choice, so I felt an overwhelming amount of responsibility.

I stayed awake at night worrying until I consulted with an attorney to draft a trust and living will. I had to make sure that my son was taken care of no matter what. A new chapter began, and I buried myself in caring for my child, working, as well as going back to school to pursue a Master's degree. Since I was so involved in the Special Education process, I decided to pursue a degree in Special Education Law.

I also took a lot of time to concentrate on my life by reading a lot of books to inspire me along with building my self-confidence. I really didn't know what the future held for me and my child, so I sort of gave up on the idea of another serious romantic relationship. I did what I always do when I don't want to face reality, which is throw myself into something. My son and my job kept me busy throughout the day and night and weekends. I didn't know how I was going to use my Master's degree, I only knew that I needed something to occupy my mind.

Keeping myself extremely busy actually worked out for several years, until one of my friends wanted me to meet her boyfriend's best friend. I started talking with this guy and we immediately clicked. We became the best of friends, we lived in different states so we communicated a lot over the telephone and that gave us the opportunity to really get into deep conversations. As the months past, we really grew close and started visiting each other on a monthly basis. It was nice and exciting in the beginning but later, the strain of a long-distance relationship were taking it's toll. I requested a transfer on my job, which wasn't located in the same city as my love interest, but it was in the same state and a two hour commute opposed to being twelve hours away.

Several months later, my job granted me a lateral position transfer. It was exciting and scary at the same time. I felt badly for my son, since his dad's family lived only three hours away and we were going to be moving 11 hours away from them. My son had lived in the same home from his birth up to that time and I worried about how he would adjust. However, I focused on the pros, such as I would have more quality time to spend with him, since my current commute to work was an hour and a half each way and which would be reduced to 15 minutes each way once we moved. Another pro was, I didn't like my son's school district and after years of fighting to get him what I felt was an appropriate education and consistently denied even with the assistance of hiring attorneys, I felt this was an opportunity for a new start. We were starting a new chapter, and I decided to go for it.

A few weeks after I received my job transfer notification, my love interest proposed marriage. It came as a total surprise to me, however, my family and friends were not surprised at all. We were on a cruise vacation with our friends who were on their honeymoon and he proposed the second night of the cruise. Thinking back now, I feel proposing while on someone else's honeymoon vacation was not the appropriate place. However, I accepted and a few weeks later I moved to a new state. We continued to date, it was still a long distance relationship, but a two hour commute was much more bearable and less costly than a 12 hour commute.

We had some issues, but they seemed to be things that we were working on. We married nine months after I moved to the area. We continued to live in separate homes, I had always refused to leave my employer. I had a child and I couldn't depend on anyone other than myself to make sure that his needs and wants were provided for. Our marriage went well for the first two years or so, until our living arrangements and other issues became a problem.

I did what I do best...I dug myself deep in my work and started a new business, a travel agency. I always loved traveling and I studied the travel business day and night. I felt that would be something that I could share with my husband. We could learn the business together and travel together. Consequently, we grew apart even more, I felt that he started to hate the real "me."

I am an introvert and I come across to many people as being really compliant and accommodating and to a degree, I am. Still, when there is something that I want to achieve, I dig my heels in and don't stop until I complete that achievement. By no means do I aim to be deceitful, but I think people see introverts as too easy going and fail to look deep at the true person. Others don't always consider that we are not going to be submissive in every situation.

That marriage ended and I learned a very valuable lesson; my *why* must be thoroughly understood and accepted. I know what my *why* is and I wake up every morning and go to bed every night with that as the ultimate goal. Twice divorced and I grieve from my loss, but I refuse to dwell in a place of grief. I continuously find strength in all the things that are going right in my life. I have a great life, I have survival in my DNA and I choose to thrive each and every day.

I find hope in each and every day of my life, I only have to look at my son to realize all that we have gone through, and this has not been an easy journey. No matter, I can still smile and continue to find ways to help others that are going through what we have and will continue to go through. I am so thankful that I continue to start new chapters, such as the nonprofit that I started last year, Cruising with Autism, Inc.

Autism has been a large part of my life for many years, I understand what families experience and I love giving back in the areas that I am most passionate. I am proving that I have been divorced, down, but I'm not dead, hope is definitely my hero. This life has not been easy, but it's so good because I have so much hope.

"Hope keeps you going when the storms of life hit. There has to be something inside that says, I have a destiny and I've got more to do." - TD Jakes

Sometimes I Feel Like a Motherless Child...

TOMIKA M. BROWN

. . . .

As I recount my almost 43-year life journey, I peel off every layer of invisible clothing that I have put on over the years that hid my scars. Thinking about how I have conveniently lodged each painful memory into the back of my brain so I can function on a daily basis, I remind myself that I am still standing. Although my knees wobble at times, I still stand.

Tears fall from my eyes and form two small puddles on my patio table as I listen to different versions of the song, "Sometimes I Feel Like a Motherless Child." This song brought many emotions forth, from anger to sorrow. I was angry that my mother left me, but in a sense I feel sorry for all she missed in my life. I feel sorry that my children have no grandmother to pass down generational wisdom. There is a part of my heart that wishes she was here for those relationships. I can still picture in my mind how much fun she would have been for my girls. I still dream, yet I had to face the fears and acknowledge the pain that had been built up and unvisited for years. I have decided to dig deep for forgiveness and break the cycle in my legacy of broken dreams.

She Didn't Quit Until She Was a Star...Her Story

As the story has been told, my mother, Venus Williams, was a smart, beautiful, courageous woman with raw talent. She was funny, the "star" of her group of friends, and a people magnet. She was so thirsty for stardom that at the age of 14, she signed up for a Miss Teenage America pageant in New York City without notifying her mother. She was a daredevil who loved the limelight, and had an undying love for my father. Her characteristics are so familiar, it feels almost as if I am talking about myself.

Experimentation with drugs, alcohol and sex only complicated her life. Pregnant with me at the tender age of 15, I am sure wasn't an easy task. My mother left me with my paternal side of the family when I was about three months old. I have been told she thought my father was cheating on her while away at college, so she made the decision to go to California to be a star. In fact her nickname became, "Star." Her journey soon led her back to New York City and continued use of drugs led to a heavy addiction to heroin.

I vaguely remember my mother calling a time or two at Christmas saying she would be coming to bring me gifts. She made promises that she never kept. The thought of her coming like Santa Claus filled me with excitement. I was restless and my heart raced with the thoughts of seeing her, bearing gifts of love for me. Then reality hit me, and the disappointment of her not coming made me feel like all hope was gone and I'd never see her again. My heart felt empty and trusting others became more difficult from fear of being let down...again and again. However, I was in a dream world when it came to my mother. Deep inside I wanted to believe she would come back for me someday.

Over the years, I developed a protective armor to guard myself from hurt and disappointment. As I have grown and shed the armor I can now say that on the outside, I hid the feelings others couldn't see, but behind the figurative metal breast plate, my heart was so broken. I could never understand why a mother would leave her child.

A Dream Deferred...His Story

From what I've been told, my father had a promising basketball career. He made the local paper almost every time he played in a game. He received a scholarship to a college in Massachusetts and he was a well-loved athlete.

69

Had he continued on that path, he may have had a chance to be in the NBA. But as we know, life has twists and turns. My father's college and pro basketball dreams were deferred when my mother left me with his parents and left to pursue her dream. My father had to drop out of college to take care of me. While my father came home and got a job to support me, in reality I was actually being raised by my grandparents. My father was physically there, but not mentally. I felt really guilty at times, thinking that I may have been the cause of his deferred dreams.

My father also used drugs which led to him to a really bad heroin addiction. He began using drugs during high school, but as his addiction worsened he began to face many unlawful situations. These legal situations almost always led to incarceration which caused him to be unavailable for the majority of my milestones like my junior high, high school, and college graduations. It killed me! Not seeing him there became just another burrowed hole in my heart. I really needed him and he did not understand that his actions were causing me to miss out on having a father.

As time went on, I realized that the choices we make not only affect ourselves, but others as well. I knew that making the right choices were so detrimental in life, as I learned that my decision making would someday affect my own children.

Nightmares and Broken Dreams.....My Story

As an only child, growing up, I had those childhood daydreams of longing to be with my mother. I wanted a relationship like my friends had with their mothers. I wanted to have a mother to laugh with me when silly things would happen, but I laughed alone. I wanted a mother to cry with me when I was so hurt deep inside, but I cried alone. I wanted a mother to shop with, go to the hairdresser with, to love me, encourage me, and show up for me. After all, that is what mothers are supposed to do! My mother never did any of those things and of course, I was usually alone. Thankfully, my grandmother helped to fill the void at times. She stepped in a lot, but she still wasn't MY mother. As a child, I spent so many nights crying myself to sleep in the dark. I buried my face into my pillow to mask the sounds of crying. I just needed to cry in an attempt to release the built up internal pain. This continues, even to this day. Although I was hurt, I felt that no one needed to know that, I needed to just handle it and keep moving silently carrying my burden.

I always say to myself I wished I had siblings I could share my feelings with, sisters or brothers to discuss "our" pain with, but now that I have really come to grips with the reality of my situation, I am happy there was no one that experienced the same internal pain I did. My parents were smart enough not to have more children who would endure such an injustice.

I believe it was kindergarten when I began to realize there was something different about me in comparison to some of my friends. On my first field trip, some of my friends' mothers accompanied them. I will always remember how lonely the ride on the bus was. Internally, I felt like an outcast. All you could hear were other kids asking their mom's for this and that as I sat alone. Although I shared a seat with a classmate, I still felt isolated. I would long for the feeling of having my mother accompany me like the other mothers did. Riding the bus with me, buying me what I wanted on the trip and waiting for others to say "Is that your mother? She is beautiful!" That day never came. In fact there were more field trips and activities at school, and the absent mother was always mine. Although I am sure there were other mothers that could not attend because of work, mine was just absent.

I experienced a bag of mixed feelings. I felt angry, jealous and abandoned all at one time. As time passed on I quickly learned to disguise my feelings by adopting my good friends' mothers as my own. Every one of my good friends will tell you that I adopted them as my sister, because I had no siblings, and their mothers because my mother was not present. So no matter who I was with, I always had a "mother" or at least someone to call mom. I began to realize that adopting mothers wasn't a permanent solution to my problem. I was still hurting, in a deep pain and adopting mothers would never cure that.

My father on the other hand was more tangible than my mother. I wanted to be able to really share with him how I was feeling without my mom. I wanted him to fix it. When I think of a father, I think of someone who is going to fix any and everything for their child. A father would never let their child hurt, and if they even felt you were hurt, someone was going to feel their wrath. Only for me, that never happened, it was just a dream.

He was physically around from time to time, but not there emotionally. Not a father. Sometimes he felt more like a big brother or uncle, than my father. I sort of fought with myself as to which role he really played. Very similar to the feelings I had with my mother, I waited in my heart for my father just to show up.

As I did with some of my friends' mothers, I observed some fathers as well. I usually looked for the type in the category that I wanted my father to fit into. He would never be them. My father was who he was, that was his character, and the character of a person seldom changes. Again, he was there at times, but emotionally he didn't show up to be the father I needed him to be. I needed him to be there to at least try to pick up some of the broken pieces my mother left me with. Couldn't he see I was hurt, struggling and deeply affected by not having my mother? My grandfather sat and listened to my concerns the few times I wanted to share my feelings, he was a placeholder, but I wanted my father to listen. As time had it, the results of my father's actions became more pieces for me to pick up. I often pondered on my situation and wondered if my dreams resulted into nightmares.

As I ventured through middle and high school my father's absence became more of an issue. My father had walked through the halls of the same schools I attended. So our family name was a quite familiar one. Everyone knew my father for his outstanding basketball career in high school. People were bursting to mention how great of a basketball player he was and inquire about where he was. That final inquiry was like pouring alcohol into my open wounds. What child wants to have to hide heartache and quickly find answers to questions that they just wanted to run away from? That was me. Just call me Miss Hyde minus the Dr. Jekyll. As I got older, I got good at telling folks that my father was in different locations around the world, not wanting to share where he really was.

College was a bit different, there were a few people from high school, but my circle was small and there weren't many who knew me or knew about my childhood circumstances. If someone knew my circumstances it was because I chose to share or they had a connection with me, like being raised by their grandparents or their parents having a drug addiction. Other than that, I was a little more carefree, but never stopped hurting. My grandparents retired from their jobs and relocated to

South Carolina during my college years. Although this was a very well deserved time for them, once again I experienced in my mind another case of abandonment. In my mind, my grandparents were supposed to be within arm's reach forever. Of course, that was not realistic.

As time went on, I realized that I needed to start to deal with the issues at hand, always wanting to know, why me? Why were MY parents not present? But as time continued to move forward I strategically became a master at pushing my pain to this little space in the back of my brain for a later visit. Just like clutter, the pain, emotions, sadness, and fear were all bagged up in that cramped area in the back of my brain. As clutter normally does, it piled up and started to cause blockage. This blockage made it painful to function. As a result, I would revisit part of the baggage, but never all at once. Revisiting pieces was much easier, it was like moving that one bag that was blocking the door which was exactly what I needed to move to function.

In my mind, I just needed to be able to get in and out of the door so to speak. I would say as long as I could make it through the day, I could hide at night when I got home. Home was that safe place for me. I could go home sit in my mirror, peel off the eyelashes, remove the wig, take off the makeup and unmask the real me, once safely behind closed doors.

Opportunities to Pick Up the Pieces

There were pivotal moments in my life where I was blessed with chances to recover those absent relationships. There are times in our lives, no matter how much we have been hurt or wronged, that we will still make decisions that no one else will approve of or ever understand.

My Mother

It has been almost 20 years since my maternal grandmother called me to sadly tell me that my mother had contracted the AIDS virus and was in her final stage of the incurable disease. This was major blow because I didn't personally know anyone with AIDS. I mean, there was Magic Johnson and he was fine. I wondered what my mother would be like. This was scary in so many different ways. The mother I never knew became the mother I would never get to know, and she was dying.

My mother had just been the highlight of Life Magazine in an article titled, "Looking for the Light" by Scott Thode. My maternal grandmother felt it was time for me to know since the article was based around her living with AIDS. I remember being in shock...emotionless. I felt the need to see her immediately. This sort of closed the gap of forever. Thoughts of being able to reunite now had a time limit called death. She was currently in the hospital in New York City. My maternal grandmother told me she had a habit of just leaving the hospital when she felt better, so I had to make it quick. I recall rushing over to see her. My ride over to see her was quiet, no music, just me and my thoughts. It was weird, I never once thought about what to say or what questions to ask, I just knew my mother was dying and I needed to see her to make sure she was alright.

Upon my arrival to the hospital, I remember it being so dark on the inside...Really different than any hospital I had ever been too...extremely dreary. When I made it to her room, it was like she saw a ghost. Her eyes were so wide that it was obvious she knew who I was. I remember her first words were "Mika, what are you doing here?" I told her I came to check on her. We looked so much alike. My heart was pounding because I really didn't know how to react or what to say. So I pulled energy from somewhere deep within to just begin talking and asking my mother was she ok.

She replied "I'm doing good, but I am ready to get out of here." There were many nurses coming in and out to monitor her. This was a very scary moment, because I didn't really know her fate. We talked for almost an hour before she drifted off to sleep. Our conversation never focused on where she had been, why she left me, or anything close to that. I really didn't know how to approach her with those questions, so I just let the day be what it was going to be. I think I was scared to hear the answers, although I knew I needed to know. Maybe that would have moved another bag.

My paternal grandmother was not pleased with my decision to take the trip, but that was one of those moments when people won't be happy with every decision you make. Although my mother left me, I knew it was not ok for me to leave her. She was dying. This was horrible. I was very sad, but never made that obvious around her when visiting. Because I was so afraid of the truth, I just tried to start from that point. As I analyze now looking back, that was not the best decision. I should have asked more questions and gotten more answers.

As my maternal grandmother warned, when my mother was better she would leave the hospital on her own. The day after our first visit she left the hospital. This kind of behavior was repeated many times. She was hard to keep track of. She would disappear onto the streets of New York. No one ever knew where she went or who she was with. It was like she vanished. This was agonizing, the possibility and fear of never seeing her again was real.

We shared a few more visits before her death. I tried to keep these visits as cheerful as possible, but it was always hard fighting back the tears. Watching her physically transform as she died was an image that will never leave my mind. She was starting to look like a skeleton. I remember her making me promise her that I would take her to Disneyland when she got out of the hospital. I also remember her making me flush her food down the toilet because she wanted to make the nurse think she ate her food. I recall telling her she needed to eat and she said "I am YOUR mother."

Our final visit together was the most painful of them all. We were all in the room with her and I stepped out to call my boss. He was really enraged that I wasn't at work. I explained to him that they did not know how much longer my mom had to live. My boss was very clear he had a company to run. So I left my mother in the hospital and drove back to New Jersey to go to work. I struggled with this decision to leave her. In my heart, I knew that it was not the right decision. Again my thoughts were, because she left me, I knew I shouldn't leave her. I was supporting myself. There was no one to call to bail me out of a bind. My grandparents were in South Carolina and on a fixed income. My grandparents saved my life, I could not expect them to take care of me if I lost my job. They had already done so much for me that I could never repay them for.

I nervously drove back to New Jersey just hoping that my mother could hang in there one more day. In my mind, I was already thinking what time I would return the next day and possibly get up the nerve to ask those important questions, but I really didn't think I would even get the chance.

I returned to work and notified my boss of my return. As soon as I sat in my desk chair, I received the call I never wanted to receive. My aunt called and said, "Mika, she's gone." It was a breath taking moment. My mother was dead. It was like someone knocked the wind out of me, the tears fell and the blame game began. I blamed myself, because I should have never left my mother. I wanted nothing more than to have a piece of a mother/daughter relationship and I didn't want to lose that dream. Everyone has their own version of why she left, but I would never get the truth from my mother.

Now, I would never hear the answers to many questions that I could only get from her. I went against everything I believed and the possibility of continuing our chapter immediately ended. I left work and went right back to New York. Crying all the way, I had asked them not to move the body so I could come back to see her as she was. I just needed to say goodbye. When I arrived the body was still there in place. I went in alone and apologized to her for leaving. Although I knew I did what I needed to do for me, I still carried the guilt in my heart that I shouldn't have left. There was a mixture of feelings and guilt because I left her. Anger because my boss needed me to come back to work. Sadness, because all chances were gone to find out anything from her mouth.

Scared, because she was really gone and that maternal attachment was left dangling.

As my dream shattered right before my eyes, I had to realize that my mother was always in search of her own dream. After she died a photo journal titled *Venus Rising* was released via the New York Times. It was an individual part of the Life Magazine article, but dedicated solely to my mother. She had become infamous for her death and not her life.

My Father

Although my father was unavailable for those important moments in my life, I still always felt that he would become available to me. That dream never dies no matter how old you get. I always wondered what I could do to save him. As a child and as I grew, he presented his situation as not being "his fault." He would always say...they framed me, they set me up, they lied...I didn't do that. This made me so angry to think that my father was in his situations because he was being set up or society just needed someone to blame and my father was the one who got the blame. It was my hope when I got older, I would become an attorney to help my father and others in similar situations be cleared. My efforts of becoming an attorney to one day save him failed when I didn't pass the test to get into law school.

Another thought came to mind when I got engaged. I knew I could never fix the past, but I wanted nothing more than to have my father walk me down the aisle during my wedding. A daughter's fairytale dream wedding. My wheels immediately began to turn and I came up with a plan to make it happen. I instantly called the prison where he was located to see if I could speak with a caseworker and explain our story. After a lengthy conversation of my father missing some important milestones in my life, I was asked to write a letter of request for this event. After reviewing my letter, the state of North Carolina accepted my request to allow him to travel to New Jersey for my wedding and like that my heart was coming together a little. Part of my dream would come to life, my father would walk me down the aisle at my wedding.

Things like this do not normally happen. I felt accomplished, like I had won a million dollars. But I also had some reservations. I always wondered if I should have made the decision for my father to walk me down the aisle. After all, we had many missing moments, and my grandfather was always there. Should my grandfather have been the one to walk me down the aisle, I questioned myself. Even though my grandfather said he was alright with my decision, in my heart I doubted the decision myself. But I forged ahead because I didn't want that dream to be lost.

As I got older, I tried to discuss my disappointments with my father, but because of so many years of lies and the blame game, I didn't trust what he said. Those conversations never really turned out to bring me the closure that I needed. As our relationship continues; we call and visit each other and I know now we can't turn back the hands of time, I will never be that little girl again.

My only wish is that my father will have a really great relationship with his grandchildren. I see the effort he puts forth, especially coming to my daughter's 5th grade graduation, when he goes to school functions, and having lunch with them at school. He tries to make things that happen, and I also see despair in his face at times that I wish I could mend. When you repair one's problems for them, they never get a chance to discover what they did wrong. We continue to work on our relationship one day at a time.

My Safety Net: The Angels Sent from God

My grandparents were my safety net. No matter how far or hard my fall, they were always there to catch me and show me how to rise again and stand tall. Although my parents lost their way in the midst of dream chasing, my grandparents immediately stepped into those roles without hesitation. My grandparents worked hard and picked up the slack to provide for me. They provided me with life skills that I continue to use to this day.

My grandmother taught me to love everyone unconditionally. My grandfather taught me the ethics behind hard work as he supported me in softball, cheerleading and all school activities. I had a really strong connection with my grandparents that I will always be eternally grateful and indebted to them for. Lodged in the back of my mind, I couldn't help but to acknowledge that they were not "my mother and father." My grandparents were my protection, in other words my safe place, and they are responsible for the woman I have become.

My Present Should Not Be a Reflection of My Past

As I think back, I was that kid, teenager and young adult who was parentless, and I didn't like that. Through all those phases of my life I always promised myself that I would NEVER be like my parents. I would never smoke, try drugs, have children before I got married and most importantly, abandon my children. I always felt I got the bad end of the stick and not many really knew exactly how that felt. Life was hard at times for me, scary, and undefined. I never knew what life would really be like for me. Relationships with men were strained and difficult at times. I always worried about if they would stay or if they were always lying about something. My past again dictated my reaction to many situations.

Just as I would adopt sisters, I would also adopt brothers. I needed some brothers just in case someone I dated go out of line, I had someone to call if I needed help. No father to call and I would never get my grandfather mixed up in some of my mess. So as I often did, I figured it out.

Finally I met this man. He was gorgeous and I immediately loved him. I was looking for that one who would protect me, never lie to me, and would never leave me. All the things I had experienced in my past. There is something about my circumstances that made me believe I always had to be strong and stand firm. I built up this outer lining to portray myself as being so strong; never letting anyone in to see the broken me, the one who was shattered into pieces because of not having a mother or stable father. These circumstances made me feel so weak. And it wasn't that I was trying to be someone else, I just put up a layer of protection so I wouldn't be hurt again. That persona affected many of my relationships.

It took us a while to really get on the same page due to some of his past relationships, as well as my tough attitude. I believed he was lying about certain things, like dealing with other women, but I knew I had to give him a chance. The more time we spent together, the more we were able to become truthful with one another about certain situations. This didn't happen instantly though. We both had to learn to that we could trust one another with our deepest fears. I eventually married this man and after thirteen years we have both grown so much. Throughout this growth we have had children. I must say this has been a really challenging task for the both of us. My husband didn't grow up with his father so we both had a sort of an internal pact that we would not allow that to happen to ours.

Having children for me was an eye opening experience. I had no mother to share my feelings with, or to help me understand what to expect. And I hated doctors' visits where they asked about my mother and father's history, because I had no clue. My pregnancies rekindled a lot of those feelings I had as a child. I had to learn how to be a mother with no guide. My grandmother was my grandmother, so I knew I would do a great job, but I had to learn on my own many things. I humbled myself to ask others things I couldn't figure it out. There were instances when my pride wouldn't allow me to ask for fear of what people might think; wondering why I couldn't just ask my mom and asking questions like, "where is your mother, or you mother didn't teach you that?" I used to worry what people thought so I tried to figure a lot on my own. Pride...it almost killed me.

When I was pregnant with my first child, my grandmother became really sick and was hospitalized for most of my pregnancy. I was so stressed knowing she was getting older, and as diabetic, her health was waning. Deep down, I knew she would not be around forever contrary to what my heart wanted to believe. My husband would drive me from New Jersey to South Carolina to see her during my pregnancy. She couldn't really speak. Her voice was a quick whisper, I kept talking to her.

I placed her hand on my stomach so she could feel her great-granddaughter. I would tell her that she couldn't leave me because I had no idea what to do with this baby. That was truly a rough time. When grandmother's leg was amputated, that was the roughest. Throughout my life, I saw her being strong and I knew she wouldn't give up. I knew she was going to be around to see her great-granddaughter. Sadly, that day never came.

About a week before she passed, my grandmother returned home from the hospital and a nurse was coming daily to check on her. As a family, we thought she would do better at home because that is where she wanted to be. During this time my husband worked nights. One particular evening I couldn't sleep at all. I felt something was wrong. I fell asleep and woke up out of a dream where I was informed that she has passed away. I was sweating. I called her the next day and she was fine. I did my best to push that idea leave my mind. Two days later I received another call I didn't want to receive. My grandmother had passed away.

I was devastated! I was torn to pieces because she was never supposed to leave me, but she had. There were so many unanswered questions, so much guilt for not being there for her, especially when she had been there for me. Again, I had to put many thoughts and feelings to the back of my mind or my pregnancy would have been at risk. The funeral was the worst, I couldn't believe she was gone. I couldn't stop crying. Again, I was left alone. That was 2004, one day before their wedding anniversary and two days before her birthday. My grandfather passed a few years ago which was another searing blow for me. May they both rest peacefully in paradise and be commended for life of sacrifice.

Motherhood has had its ups and downs and has made me extremely emotional and protective of my children to a point that I have separation anxiety. I really worry about their thoughts and their feelings. I want my children to feel safe always knowing I will be there to support them. I want them to always feel that I love them and want them around. I want them to always feel that mommy keeps her promises. I want them to take comfort in knowing that if they need me, I will always be there.

I desired real hard core honesty, no matter how much it would hurt, when it came to learning about my parents.

I needed to know the truth for me. I tried many different roads for the truth, grandmothers, aunts and uncles, but I always received their versions of a story, and not just the plain old truth. Many versions contradicted others and just didn't add up. I felt like I had been misled and my trust issues grew. No one ever just said what happened.

Eventually, I found an uncle and my godmother who didn't dance around the truth with me. Although they didn't know the beginning to end of my parent's lives, they were able to give me a peek into who my parents were. I was a woman who had a mother and a father, yet didn't know who they were. This was and still is a deep rooted empty feeling. I need to know them. The emptiness will always remain a void.

There Are Lessons at the End of Every Story

Although this struggle within me has gone on for many years and continues, I have faith that there is always survival in the struggle, the sun still shines, and the rain will eventually go away. I have learned many lessons along my long journey and I challenge you:

- To be real with yourself; know what you want and what you don't want. Recognize what you do want may not always be the best for you. Although I wanted my parents to be present, I have to realistically ask myself, as I look at my life now, would that have been the best option. Being solely with either one of my parents could have resulted in me not being who I am today. It may have also not allowed me to be a help to so many of my students I have helped.

- When there's a lot to deal with, you can't handle too much at once. In order to survive and function in your day-to-day living, try relocating the pain to the back of your mind and revisit it later. This can provide time for you to process it when you're ready. Then peel back the layers and become transparent enough to help yourself seek forgiveness.

- Don't let your past define your future.....break the cycle...build your legacy... I promised myself that I would NEVER BE LIKE MY PARENTS. We make pacts with ourselves throughout our lives, sometimes we keep them and sometimes we don't. Often as we grow, pacts become unrealistic or unattainable, but through determination, I have been able to break the cycle and build my legacy with my children.

You have to be willing to be transparent to begin the transition...get naked or you will remain stuck! With me what you see is what you get. I am not perfect, nor do I pretend to be, I am rough around the edges. In order to begin to declutter your inner pain, heartache, sadness and fear, you have to unleash your faith and begin to get naked emotionally...starting with YOU first. You cannot share your story unless you come to terms with your story.

An Angry Letter to My Sperm Donor

TAMEKA L. WILLIAMSON

The Revelation

*I*t was an afternoon meeting, one weekday in October 2007 when my perspective and life would forever change. Little did I know, it be for the better. The entire year of 2007 overall was one of the toughest years of my life, filled with an incredible amount of hurt and pain. You see, I lost my really good friend, sister and fellow choir member, Rainy, as well as started working for the worst boss ever, who made it her mission to make my life hell! We were literally like oil and water...we simply didn't mix!

Throughout my career, I had the opportunity to work for top-tier Fortune 25 companies in interesting roles. For the most part, they were just jobs to me until I joined a major retailer. Initially, I LOVED my job and the company.

This was the company that went beyond the call of duty to help me and others recover from the aftermath of Hurricane Katrina. The values I were sold on during the interviewing process were actually manifested in the flesh. Never had I seen that before.

At the same time, I was making great career moves, getting exposed to great opportunities and was in a position where I was not only making a difference for my staff, but for the company as well. I was classified as a "Hi-Po" employee, that references a high potential employee. Hi-Po employees are individuals classified as promotable and considered for maximum raises, bonuses and special opportunities.

Unfortunately, my glory days came to an unexpected screeching stop a few years later. My hard work and reputation as a strong contributor seemed to have been ignored by some and I couldn't figure out why. It was like I fell from grace, but I didn't do anything to warrant the descent. That is the point where my love for my job began to diminish. Have I involuntarily moved from being on top of the world to being on the bottom of somebody's shoe? There were people I helped get to where they were enjoying living out their careers, while nobody from my team stepped up to advocate for or support me.

There was a changing of the guards in leadership and various selfish motives were being played out. Other members of my team were able to see their career aspirations being fulfilled. On the contrary, mine were being stifled by individuals I once trusted. When the environment began to change, my daily struggle to go to work also began. So, I leaned on the prayers, encouragement and advisement of some close friends. One of them was my friend, Rainy. She was my anchor; she encouraged me, gave me perspective, and helped me to keep going every day. Rainy urged me not give up. She would remind me God was preparing me for something bigger and not to give up. Whenever I felt like screaming, walking out, or was just plain ol' discouraged, I would call her, text her or she would send me a message encouraging me.

Then the paradigm shifted in an unexpected way and I ended up in a role I was overqualified for, wasn't challenged by and the boss from hell. I accepted the role just to have a job, not knowing how it would change my life for the worst. My boss did everything in her power to make my life miserable, being spiteful in many instances to break me down. I was determined to fight my way out of that situation.

Sometimes God lets things happen to you because He sees where you are going. He is not concerned about your comfortability. He is more concerned about your growth and development. This is the result of me becoming comfortable and settled where I was. God commanded more, He had to shake me up. So, the agitation was like none other. A few weeks after starting my new role, Rainy was promoted to heaven suddenly and unexpectedly. It all happened the night before my birthday and housewarming party, where she was one of the planners and caterers. As you can imagine, I was devastated!

You see this was the second birthday in a row where I lost someone I cared about around my birthday. Instead of celebrating my birthday, I had to deal with grief and funerals. The previous year for my 30th birthday, a milestone birthday where BIG plans were made, one of my line sisters was murdered. Needless to say, that grand celebration never happened. I ended up helping to plan and participate in the homegoing celebration of my line sister, whom I had just communicated with the day before her demise about us celebrating my birthday and her admission into medical school. Two sad and tragic moments two years in a row around my birthday crippled me for the next two years causing me not to celebrate my birthday because I was fearful about planning celebrations. Afraid someone I loved would die if I did.

We are not supposed to just go through life, but actually grow through life. So, this was my time to be pruned, which is very uncomfortable and painful, but necessary. Because I am a natural introvert, I keep to myself with private matters and don't necessarily share my feelings; especially in the workplace. I would have to really trust someone to share that type of information with them. Although I was going through a highly emotional time, I had to process it in my own way and that took a while. It also meant, I could not grieve publicly at work. Not sharing my feelings about the death of my friend with my coworkers and processing my grief quietly by focusing on my work was used against me.

While my new boss was on leave, the "fill-in" person, who was intimidated by me and my accomplishments used it against me. She couldn't understand me, nor did she try. Our first interaction started off with her commenting on how she knew I was overqualified for the job, looking at the wealth of knowledge I had based on my previous role and resume. As it turned out, my credentials were more substantial than hers. We were about the same age, just not the same race. As she was learning the role being the new person on the team, I didn't wait for her to teach me. I figured things out for myself.

It didn't make sense for the blind to lead the blind. As a result, she painted me in an unfavorable light, a disservice to who I really was, to my new boss. This lead my new boss to believe I was not a team player because I didn't ask a lot of questions, I wouldn't share personal information with her or the team, wouldn't to do lunch with them much, and completed my work away from the group.

Instead of my new boss giving me a fair shot, she took the words and actions of an insecure manager and ran with it as the true gospel. It was a prime example of giving a person power who let it go to their head. Ultimately, the stress from working in the hostile work environment she created led me to take a stress leave from my job for nine weeks in 2007. Not only did I not have the time to fully grieve, I had to fight for my career. It was the first time in my life I felt that defeated.

I was always strong-minded and confident in what I had to offer. But, I had lost sight of who I was, allowed this downfall to damage my spirit, get in my head and it almost broke me. I would cry daily on my way to and from work and sometimes in the middle of the day. Finally, I got to the point where enough was enough and that is when I went on leave. All the while, I was suffering in silence, masking the pain every time I ministered through song each week at church on the Praise Team and in the choir. I was basically hiding my pain from the outside world, walking around broken on the inside with daily thoughts of giving up. Oh, I didn't tell you, I was appointed to the Praise Team a week after Rainy passed, filling her spot. Wow, music is my passion and my ministry. Here I am, having the awesome privilege to serve and lead worship, what an honor. Yes it was, but it took me a long time to adjust because I felt I replaced my sister which only adding to my emotions.

I remember telling God, "Take me now! I'd rather be at home with you in peace than to go through this emotional pain anymore." God wasn't having it! He began to speak to me in various ways and reveal to me who I was in Him and let me know that this was part of my process. He was taking me to the next level. He had a purpose for me, work for me to do and people for me to help. It was now time for me to reclaim my power and declare victory over the situation.

The reality is this...whenever you allow another person to dictate how you respond to a situation, they have power over you. This should not be. You should not give another two-legged human being this much power and control over your life. Once I realized that, I began regaining my strength to believe in myself once again and fight for my place to do what God fashioned me to do.

The other side was realizing everything I do should be pleasing to only two people: myself and God. Who cares what other people think? The words of a former mentor came to me, "Tameka, you are a statuesque, smart, black female engineer and that threatens many. You can't control that, because it's who you are. You must do your best work regardless because you work for God, not man." I have to constantly remind myself of these profound words spoken to me back in 2001. With this, I had an epiphany after one of Bishop's sermons concerning the reasons things happen to you. Basically, I can be the best at what I do and people will still dislike me. Jesus was perfect and they disliked him. What makes me different? These three points stuck with me from that moment:

1. Things happen as a result of something you've done or didn't do.

2. Things happen because people just don't like you.

3. Things happen just because.

Regardless of the reason, I knew that I had the power to dictate how I would respond. Even though I know everything that happens to me has a purpose, I still feel the need to ask, "Why me?" I had to reevaluate that changing it to, "Why not me?" What makes me exempt? It may be weird, but I had to realize that I was chosen for this challenge because God loves me that much and He trusts me enough to handle it. This was my reality check, a new perspective on life. Not only was I "chosen," but it was part of the process God was sending me through to take me to a new place of greatness.

Being on a paid leave required me to get approval from a psychologist, a therapist who could diagnose the need for a leave. From there, I would have to agree to see a psychiatrist on a weekly basis, so they can prescribe medication to ease me through the process. My initial meeting was with a female psychologist. After sitting in this lady's office reluctantly and only so I could get my leave approved, God gave me the revelation of my life. This revelation shattered the thoughts I had that only "crazy" and "unstable" people visit the "head" doctors.

It was after my assessment, answering what I perceived to be basic questions, she told me earth shattering news that hit me to my core: "Your life is out of balance! You are consumed with work and church. That is it. I believe this is because you have a drive for success due to you overcompensating for not feeling 'good enough' in the eyes of others because your dad rejected you as a child. So, you have a strong disposition about yourself that keeps you on top and in a place where you don't allow yourself to be vulnerable or dependant on others. You've worked hard to accomplish all that you have and value trust a lot. Therefore, you fight to protect that. Being out of balance, you have no outlet for countering the challenges at work."

WOW! Where did this woman come from and how did she figure all this out in such a short amount of time? I never thought about these things before, but it definitely struck a chord with me. I grew uncomfortable, I didn't understand why.

Looking back over my life, I had always been successful. Graduating as a Mechanical Engineer and then attaining my MBA in Management, I was determined to be a force to be reckoned with. Every career decision I made catered to this mission. If I felt a job was not challenging me, I would move on to another job. People around me couldn't get why I wouldn't settle for just making a high salary. I needed more than that! I needed to feel like I was making a difference...adding value, yet learning at the same time.

Working as an engineer was no easy feat. Being an educated, considered smart, quick on my feet, and statuesque, African American female with a strong personality seemed to inspire self-doubt in others. There were many times in the workforce I was faced with situations where those folks second-guessed me in an attempt to discredit me.

Early in my career, I didn't care because I didn't take no crap. My strong demeanor, tenacious and determined spirit was what I needed to fight for my place in Corporate America. Unfortunately, this approach oftentimes was unsettling for the men and the few women around me. What was a girl to do? I was confident in who I was in the corporate space because my work ethic was second to none and my commitment was to build and maintain a strong reputation. I did that, which opened doors for me.

At the same time, it didn't come easy because I was not the typical passive, in-the-box thinking female they were accustomed to dealing with. Being a puppet and playing the corporate game was never my thing. I called a spade a spade. Two plus two is four and nothing else, I don't care how you try to spin it.

Defying the odds and being a unique individual was what I knew to do. Who needed to kiss babies and suck up to the boss when you worked hard, gave 200%, delivered results and knew how to lead? Where is the next problem for me to solve? That is what I asked. I had to do to stand out. Hard work pays off! Let your work speak for yourself. Be the "go to" person. Going above and beyond couldn't possibly be a bad thing. Everyone wants someone committed, not willing to back down from a challenge. Right? Well, I was that chick!

As you can probably tell, my focus was always on my professional career and never my personal life. I had never equated that my desire to be the best professionally was motivated by an absentee man who I had referred to as my sperm donor. I thought my determination as a young adult, and not getting pregnant as a teenager, like my peers, was a great thing. I felt my desire to go to college and do more than others in my family and neighborhood was what I was supposed to do. I figured me giving more than others was because my expectations were much higher.

In my mind, I didn't want to settle for less and that was just who I was. I was convinced that if I played big, I would win big. That's how life played out for me until 2007. Who cared that my biological father was not there for me growing up? God sent me a stepfather who I grew to love and who I eventually realized was a blessing to my mom and me. He is who I identify with as my father. I overcame that void, that rejection, that loss...or so, I thought.

Truth be told, the challenging time at my job led me to a place of vulnerability in a space that was uncomfortable and foreign to me. Overachievers and overcomers have the ability to conquer that which they are faced with. I wasn't conquering this situation; it was getting the best of me. Furthermore, it wasn't someone I trusted who led me to the light and made it more acceptable for me to process because I knew they loved me and cared about my future. It was a stranger who I had just met, taking a peak into my past and calling me on the carpet. This forced me to face an internal turmoil that I didn't really know existed. This internal battle had been orchestrating my decisions my entire life. It was like the scene from *The Color Purple* when Ms. Sofia asked Harpo "Harpo, who 'dis woman?"

Who was this woman who told me my burning desire to succeed and be the best was me trying to show my sperm donor I was GOOD ENOUGH...I was the BEST...I DESERVED the best...I didn't need him because I worked hard and made it happen for myself with the help of God and my family! Who would have thought being an overachiever would cause me to face my inner most struggles?

I was shaken at my core and had to determine what this all meant and more importantly how to move forward. It was my new challenge. One unlike any of the others faced before in my life. It was time to do some serious personal work, but I was ready!

The Rejection

"The DNA Blood test results says she is 99.99% your child," has resonated in my mind since I was 6 years old...I am now 39 years old. This information was revealed when my mom decided to pursue child support for the second time. In her first attempt when I was a baby, she walked out of court telling my sperm donor screw him and she didn't need him. When the judge told my sperm donor the results of the paternity test, he still denied me as his child. My mom was so hurt. How could science say I belonged to him and he *still* ignored me, his own flesh and blood? Was I not good enough? Pretty enough? Special enough? These are the questions and feelings I've felt most of my life. If I'm truly honest, they try to rear their ugly head even today. This was the ultimate rejection!

When I was younger I would tell myself, "I don't have a father. I am a gift from God to my mother because she was told she couldn't have kids. She just had a sperm donor to make it happen." Because of his absence, I grew up doubting myself, not feeling worthy, and felt like the odd ball amongst my friends. I was a tall girl, with long legs, arms and fingers that caused me to stand out in all my classes. Kids being kids, they sometimes teased me for having long fingers, being dark and tall. They would say I had ET fingers, pick on me for being tall and lanky, also calling me names like horse, darky, ugly and moose.

As you can imagine, my self-confidence was pretty low. In fact, I thought I was the ugliest person among all my friends, especially when it seemed as though all the guys paid them more attention. So, I had to figure out ways to be cool. Unfortunately, this resulted in me almost losing my life due to me putting myself in some precarious situations. You see, after getting picked on and beat up, I had to learn to defend myself physically and stand up for myself mentally. I became a tough person.

Singing was my other outlet; I even faced rejection there. Coming from a musical family having my grandfather as the pastor of our church, I thought I would get to sing like my mom. Well that didn't happen, I was not one of the "favorites" of the choir director. It didn't matter that my grandfather was the Pastor. I was still shut down, constantly rejected and nobody really came to my defense as I expected them to. I was more comfortable singing around my friends because they were more accepting. It was something I could do that they couldn't. In my mind, they had the looks and were lighter than I, but I had the voice. In my mind, this was another area in my life that I put my heart into and still was rejected. This further impacted my self-confidence. I was left to my own devices by creating an environment where "I thought" I could be viewed as a champion in the eyes of others. That place was centered on me building a tough mentality in school and amongst my friends.

Establishing and keeping up this image was part of who I thought I needed to become to get noticed and be included. It got so bad that I began fighting boys to prove how tough I was, wrestling and playing basketball with the guys, and even carry a key chain full of padlocks in the event I got into a fight or someone tried to jump me. As a matter of fact, after wearing dresses to my Catholic school every day in fifth and sixth grade showed me just how hard it was to fight in them. In seventh grade and beyond, I refused to wear dresses so I could be ready to throw blows if someone came my way or looked at me funny.

Writing this story, I chuckle at how foolish I was. It makes me thankful God was protecting me in the midst of my buffoonery and ignorant behavior. One particular time that comes to mind was going to a football game with one of my BFF's and her cousins. We got into a BIG brawl. We basically jumped this girl and I don't really know why. The bottom line was, It WAS NOT my fight to begin with, but I contributed because it was my crew which it added to my reputation for being "hard".

What did I know about being "hard" anyway? I had two hard working parents, a mother who did not play, and attended a college prep school, also known as "the nerd school", where I was a scholar athlete involved in National Honor Society, Leadership/Community Clubs, Basketball, Track, Cheerleading, and Drill Team. Those who know my mom, know that she would have killed me for engaging in such activities and probably would have beaten the desire to be "hard" right out of me. It was as if I was living a double life, serving as a double agent because my mom didn't know half of the things I did. If she did, I might not be alive to this day. But God!

After the brawl, we had to scatter like rats and run for our lives because the girl came back with her crew who then came after us. That was the first time I ever jumped a fence and actually was scared out of my mind. My heart was beating so fast! I experienced fear like never before. I thought I saw my life pass before my eyes. Thankfully, God covered me in the middle of my foolishness. I later found out that somebody from her crew came up to our high school looking for us with a gun to kill us. It seemed like literally dodged a bullet.

Clearly, this reckless behavior was going to take me down the wrong path if changes were not made. It was the tough love and intervention of one of my basketball coaches, Ms. Worthy and one of my beloved math teachers, Mrs. Cooper, God bless her soul, who changed my path and life. In my normal "tough" mode, I was getting ready to fight an archrival outside Mrs. Cooper's class, but she intervened, pulled us into her classroom and had a serious conversation with us. This feud had been going on for three years between my group from the class of '94 and class of '93 crew.

Mrs. Cooper basically spoke into my life at that moment and told me, "You are better than this!" and went further to say that was not how young ladies carried themselves. I could do and be whatever I wanted, but fighting was not going to get me there. I never got to thank her for saving my life. She passed the following year from cancer.

That was a turning point for me...for all of us. Although her presence was missed, her legacy lived on through us as we let the feud go and became more amicable towards one another. Thank you again, Mrs. Cooper, hope you were proud of us!

Mrs. Cooper's talk got me determined to do something positive. That was around the time I made the decision to become an engineer. Eventually my energy went into becoming more of an overachiever and succeeding by any means necessary. Basically, I ended up trading one vice for another. You see I always worked hard and stayed active and involved in leadership type organizations. Remember, I had a mother who didn't play and she regulated everything! I played with some fire, but that fire was one I didn't stoke too often. I wasn't crazy!

Looking back on the foolish actions I took just to fit in and be popular were all temporary. The reality of my low self-esteem was still present and the self-doubt remained in most of the things I did or attempted to do from sports, drill team, leadership clubs to relationships. The more I doubted myself or felt others didn't approve, the more effort and energy I put towards changing that view.

The First Encounter

Let's fast forward to Labor Day weekend 1994. It was my first year in college, early Saturday morning at 7 a.m., the phone rang and it was a "ghost" in the form of my sperm donor. The voice on the other end of the phone said, "Hey! I got your letter." There I was 18 years old and it was the first time in my life I have ever heard this man's voice, talked to him or had any interaction of any kind. He was not calling to see how the daughter he denied and failed to take care of 18 years ago was doing. Nope, he called because I sent him and his wife a scathing letter filled with a lot of anger and venom.

Before I started college, I wanted to send my sperm donor a letter to get some things off my chest as a started this new phase in my life. As I wrote the letter, I imagined what I would say if he was standing in front of me. From there, all the anger and rage I felt inside came up and out, spilling onto the paper. The letter was filled with things like: "How can you be a Christian and Deacon and you have a child you don't even know or take care of? You and your wife are just hypocrites and sorry individuals. Sending child support is not taking care of a child. You couldn't even do that right. What kind of woman would marry and stick with a man like you – one who doesn't take care of his responsibility? She's just as bad as you!"

You see, there were times when he would go missing and the child support agency couldn't find him to make him pay. Every time they found him, they sent us his contact information. This time, my mom shared it with me in the event I wanted to reach out to him because she felt I was old enough to handle the information. She also thought it was important to make the attempt to connect with him because I had other siblings I should get to know.

Being one who didn't back down from a challenge, I did just that. As I stated, there were things I had to say. Besides, I wanted to let him how I felt about him and how he repudiated his responsibility. I absolutely had to let him know how angry I was, how I basically hated him, how I made it in spite of feeling the pain he subjected me to for 18 long years. My mom was glad that I wrote the letter, although neither of us thought we would get a response. It was more of a therapeutic release for me when I mailed the letter. Little did she know, it was not the type of letter she would approve of because I did not mince words, using language that was inappropriate for any child to say to an adult. Thankfully, she never saw the letter.

Even though I was wracked with anger and pain, there was still a yearning to get to know who my father was, while letting him see how I still made it without his help. So, I was more surprised and nervous when he called, then angry as a result. As you can imagine, it was very awkward with moments of silence at times. I remember him recalling parts of the letter and asking me about them then tell me how they provoked him to call me. He could sense the anger in my message, but it also struck a negative chord with his wife. Needless to say, she was not happy with the things I had to say about her. Nonetheless, this opened the door for there to be follow up conversations, which started with weekly/bi-weekly early Saturday morning calls.

He was the only person to call at 7 a.m on a Saturday. In the process of us getting to know one another, I found out I had two older brothers in addition to the son and daughter he had with his wife. All of a sudden, I went from being my mom's only child with a younger cousin who was raised as my brother (my mom's deceased baby sister's son) and four stepbrothers to having an additional, two big brothers and a younger brother and sister.

Here is the kicker, one of my older brothers is only eight days older than me. That's right! We are the same age, born the same month, in the same city, eight days apart. Needless to say, we were excited to meet one another and instantly became inseparable. It was because of my oldest brother's advice that I made the decision to meet the "sperm donor" for the first time two years later. Although, we would talk, I was still bitter and angry. The feelings of rejection and hurt ran deep. He still needed to apologize to me and work to earn my forgiveness!

The Path Towards Forgiveness

Forgiveness was taught to me growing up in the church and I knew it was something I had to do. Let us just say, it's easier said than done. We can repeat the Lord's Prayer 100 times, but it means nothing if you don't actually do it. It just wasn't an easy or quick process, especially for me. At that point in my life, because of the ingrained hurt and pain I encountered, I held grudges for a long time. I had to really pray, talk to mentors who I trusted or who had gone through a similar situation. Then I had to pray and pray some more, then pray again.

There were countless walls built up around me and my heart that served as my protective barrier. When people met me, they would encounter my defensive side until I felt comfortable enough to let them in. I remember one of my friends told me in college, "T, you are an attractive person, but you have this unapproachable demeanor that scares people off. It makes them not want to approach you or get close."

In my mind, if I didn't set expectations or allow people to get close enough to hurt me, I would save myself that pain. Ultimately, that frame of mind allowed me to minimize room for disappointment, or so I thought. My reality was every time I allowed someone to get close or trusted someone, they ended up hurting me, disappointing me and/or failed to honor their word. If I can't trust you and what you say, I don't have time for you and don't need you.

What I thought was protection was really driving me into a place of isolation. This is what I later realized happens when you let resentment live in your heart. It will take up residence and lead you down a path of destruction and unproductive behaviors. This is not what I wanted for myself! So, I had to find a way to move forward, past these hurts and pain. I'm so glad, God saw my tears, heard my cry and led the right people to help me through this difficult journey.

As I mentioned before, letting go was not easy for me. But, forgiveness is not for the other person, it is for you. I had to reclaim my life and move forward. There were two wonderful ladies sent my way who shared with me their paternal struggles and journey to forgiveness. They were able to relate to my struggle and counsel me, step-by-step to the place God wanted me to be. Because of their advice, constant prayers, as well as my willingness to listen, my heart began to soften towards my sperm donor. God was able to use me.

I was not only able to forgive him, but my actions reflected this forgiveness as well. One major shift came when I realized, that I could not expect nor dictate what he should be doing. Every time I did that, I walked away disappointed. My initial thoughts were, "You haven't done anything for me for 20 plus years, the least you can do is be here now and try to make up for lost time." This attitude prevented full forgiveness, setting our relationship up for failure.

Eventually, I came to understand that he didn't have the capacity to do what I thought should have come naturally. For example, when I was unemployed twice within three years, it was natural for my mom to call and ask if I needed help. Yet when going through the most difficult times in my life, he didn't show up in that way. You see, I went from a six figure salary, two homes and more than $30k in savings to being homeless with zero savings.

When I was down and out, it was my mother, father and grandparents who showed up for me. They made sacrifices to make sure I was taken care of. Heck, I even had friends who gave me more support than my sperm donor did. As a result, I got frustrated and cried many tears asking, "Why can't he step up and be a father to me for once in my life?" God gave me an answer. Of course it wasn't what I wanted to hear, yet it made sense.

It was unrealistic and really unfair of me to expect him to do the same thing my parents had done. We didn't have that the same connection and love that existed between my parents, grandparents, friends and me. Yes, he was my "dad," but we were not connected in a way a father and daughter should be for him to have automatic caretaker thinking like he did with my younger siblings. You'd think it would come to him instinctively, however, that was assuming, which was just unrealistic. Once I understood this, it made a difference for me, because it lessened the stress I put myself through, decreased my frustration and it allowed me to move closer to a place of true forgiveness by accepting him just as he was.

I learned that healing and forgiveness should not be about, "What he could do for me now," rather than be about the bigger picture...relationships, family history, and establishing new experiences. I also learned that it is possible to give without loving, although you can't truly love without giving. I had to let him be his authentic self and give authentically, not out of obligation and guilt. The two don't have the same effect.

Consequently, I was eventually able to graduate from calling the sperm donor by his first name then eventually to calling him "Dad" without any angst and to now being able to say, "I Love You" and mean it. There is one thing anyone who knows me can say, you will not get me to say a thing unless I truly mean it and believe it. So, when I say something, take notice because it has meaning and it was said with intention. Now, this doesn't mean everything was perfect between us, but it was a start towards being a work in progress.

One of the greatest wins for me in forgiving my sperm donor was that it gave me an inner peace I didn't have before. Now, the protective walls I had built over decades started to come down at one time, at least most of them. I can now begin to walk in my newfound place of peace and healing. This situation was really just one component of the healing process, a major one nonetheless. The new foundation has been established, giving us room to build and move forward stronger....a fresh start.

Healing of a Family

Forgiveness is truly a process, but one worth taking. Now that my sperm donor and I have found common ground, we have been able to spend more time together. On top of that, my extended family has grown and immediate family has gotten stronger. We are not where I would like to see us, but we definitely are not where we used to be. All I've been through, has taught me to appreciate the small things. Meeting my aunts and uncles, attending and celebrating my dad's 60th birthday, going to family reunions, wishing my step-mother congratulations on her degree and having those family moments are what matters the most.

Life is too short to focus on what didn't happen. We can't change the past, but we can use it as a lesson learned on how to move forward better and stronger. So, next steps for me is to unite my family for us to have a heart to heart conversation about the past, face it and address it, release any lingering pain or issues, then establish a common ground we can move forward from having finally putting a lid on the past. This way we can progress without feeling the need to throw the past in one another's face. Now, I'm in a place of healing, deliverance, and restoration.

Through Rain Comes Shine

TALISHA SHINE

. . . .

As I stared down at the double lines on the test stick, all I could think about was what was I was going to do now. My pulse quickened each time the question flashed through my head. An instantaneous and overwhelming weakness kept me from moving away from the counter where the EPT box and instructions were lying. I was a soon-to-be 30-year old single woman, with a great job, wonderful relationship and pregnant. And I felt completely helpless and fearful.

Dialing my boyfriend's number, I told him that the pregnancy test was positive to which he replied, "Positive you are or not?" I could feel myself shutting down and didn't want the conversation to degrade into me incoherently sobbing into the phone so I mustered the strength to reply, "Positive that I'm pregnant!" The angst in my voice couldn't be disguised and as he attempted to probe me further, I knew that I wouldn't be able to respond. He asked me if I wanted him to come to the house. I immediately told him that he didn't have to come and instantly hung up the phone.

I could barely handle this moment for myself, let alone be conscious of his feelings. I wanted to protect and shield him from the pending fallout that was overtaking me. As I wiped tears from my eyes, I hurriedly hung up the phone to contemplate my next move, I busied myself with neatly folding up the instructions and reinserting them into the box. Looking for anything that I could do except think was all I wanted at that moment. Yet those two bright pink lines were like a flashing red light signaling that immediate action needed to be taken.

The blare of my door buzzer startled me and I flinched before running to press the button. I instinctively knew it was Ahmed. Apparently my quivering voice must have betrayed the logical words that were always my go-to defense. What would I say to him? What would his reaction be? Would he be upset? Question after question flooded my mind as I opened the door. The handsome face that I adored looking at for the past two years had an unfamiliar gaze and the concern in his eyes instantly caused my heart to sink further. The minute I heard his voice asking me if I was okay, I could no longer contain myself and fell to the floor to weep. Looking up at him, I couldn't discern his thoughts as he stared at me seemingly in disbelief.

"I've never seen you like this", he said.

"You've never seen me pregnant!" I sobbed. As he knelt down to sit next to me, I could feel my body beginning to shake uncontrollably.

"It will be okay", he repeated over and over again as he wrapped his arms around me.

"But how? How would this be okay?" I couldn't begin to understand how he could confidently utter those words. We had previously discussed children during the first year of our relationship. He had told me that he had always wanted a daughter and had even chosen a name for her when he was a child. I found it odd that he was so definitive about being a father because I was so disconnected from thoughts of parenthood. He was six years younger than me, yet seemed to have such a clear vision for his life. And that very clarity seemed to be the foundation for his reassurance. Although I continued to cry throughout the night, we began to formulate a plan between my tearful bouts. His words soothed me and decisive tone consoled me. As I drifted into sleep, a calm settled in. I would have never guessed that this was would be the brief calm before the storm.

I spent the next morning crying, yet filled with resolve. The plan was to contact my consulting firm to schedule a discussion regarding upgrading my insurance package. Then I would inform my employer of my pregnancy. I'd work my way through contacting my friends and then I would tell my mother. I purposefully saved the hardest for last. I felt that I needed to have things under control on the job front and the support of my friends before broaching my pregnancy with her. With my mental checklist in order, I went about the work of making calls and scheduling appointments. The end of the day brought a level of satisfaction that gave me hope that this just might work. Yet my hopes were quickly dashed when I met with my consulting firm the next afternoon.

Leaving work to meet with my consulting representative, I inquired if anyone wanted me to bring them anything back for lunch. My question was met with evasive no's and cowardly head shrugs. It was odd, but I dismissed it as I locked my workstation. I told my cubicle partner that I would return shortly and headed out. When I arrived at the office I was politely greeted and escorted to the main conference room. I had rehearsed what I was to say and ran the lines through my head as I waited for my rep.

When he entered, I instantly noticed that he had a folder in his hands. I assumed this to be the paperwork regarding my new policy. Yet once he sat down and began to speak, I was totally unprepared. "Effective immediately you are terminated from your position. The contract has expired and the client doesn't wish to renew it," spewed from his mouth like a bad-tasting drink. I blinked several times to focus on his expression but, his face remained blank.

"Please don't take this personally" he quipped. "The position has just become high profile and now requires a full-time employee." Completely stunned, I could barely find the words to speak.

"Can I be considered for a full-time position?" I asked.

He quickly responded with "No." He then proceeded to request that I provide him with my key card, badge, and company cellphone. He advised me that I would not be able to return to work and that they would have my things boxed up and someone would deliver them to me. My shock instantly shifted into anger and I snatched my cellphone from the table and phoned my boyfriend who also worked with me. With my eyes firmly affixed on my rep and in a sharp tone, I informed Ahmed that I had been fired and that he needed to come and get me. I also told him that he would need to bring all my things, as I was no longer permitted to enter the building.

His reaction only fueled my indignation and I continued to fully converse with him repeating the details as they had been told to me yet with much spite and sarcasm. "Just come and get me now" were my final words as I pounded the 'End Call' button. My consulting rep had a worried look on his face and nervously retorted that I hadn't been fired, but rather the contract was simply not being renewed. My uplifted arched eyebrow coupled with a guttural, "uh-huh" made him shift in his seat.

I turned my eyes back to the phone and called my co-worker. She immediately picked up and began telling me that there were people at my desk taking things. I told her that I had been fired and I wanted her to retrieve all my notebooks from my desk. She responded, "Those were the very first items that they took!" She then proceeded to tell me that right after I left the office, my team was told that I wouldn't be returning and if asked by clients to tell them that I was on vacation.

She, too, had been fired and was told after the team announcement. Infuriated by her comments, I abruptly stood up from the table jolting my rep from his chair. Once he gained his footing, he hastily asked for me to sign the documents, which were in the folder on the table. He told me to take my time and read through them and if I had any questions to feel free to call the office. My death stare obviously communicated my sentiments to his statements as he nervously nodded and left the conference room.

Grabbing the folder, I glanced over its contents before stuffing the papers back inside. I was unable to focus and knew that I wasn't in the right state of mind to sign anything. I noticed my car outside and with that, I grabbed the folder and stomped out of the conference room. The receptionist stood up and before she could speak I said, "I'll review these and have them dropped off once I've signed them." I forcefully pushed the door open and raced to the car.

My disbelief and anger played tug-o-war with my thoughts leaving me feeling exhausted and defeated. "This just can't be happening!" was all I kept repeating as we drove home. I wanted Ahmed to stay with me, but I knew that he had to go back to work. I didn't want him to worry so I told him I would be fine, I would just take a nap. It took everything in me to let go of him when he hugged and kissed me goodbye.

As soon as I closed the door, I began to cry. It poured out of me until I was breathless. Clutching the pillow so tightly, I felt that if I let go I would free fall into despair. My life was unraveling quickly. In just a mere week, I found out I was pregnant, lost my job, and would be turning 30 in a few days. This was definitely *not* a part of the plan! None of it! I had no idea of what to do or even how to devise a new plan. With the previous plan nullified and fear swiftly taking hold, I felt truly lost. All I could do now was find peace in sleep.

The next few days I spent contemplating what I was going to do with myself. I had finally brought myself to read through all the paperwork and was hit with yet another reality – I was no longer insured. With my first prenatal visit scheduled, I was quite concerned with how I would be able to cover the costs of prenatal care and my delivery. My gynecologist recommended a superb OB/GYN that he thought would be right for me. Although I was very anxious, she reassured me that everything would be fine and thoroughly reviewed the payment options that I would be afforded. Having completed the money conversation, she proceeded with my examination. Her soft voice was immediately drowned out by the loud throbbing heartbeat of my baby. The strength of those beats brought tears of joy to my eyes. I would forever recall that moment and draw my own strength from my child's heart.

As I left the doctor's office, I felt a renewed sense of self. Not knowing what lay ahead of me, I felt a level of determination well up inside me. My primal survival instinct brought a keen clarity that I had truly never experienced until that day. While I still felt fear and apprehension, I also had a sense of purpose that I had not had before. The thought of being someone's mother struck a chord in me that I never knew existed. The reverberations continued to ripple through me for days to come.

As my first trimester drew to a close, I had settled into a new routine that included searching for a job and all things baby. Being the information junkie that I am, I combed through article after article about pregnancy, labor, delivery you name it. TLC's *The Baby Story* became my favorite show. Since I had crying fits daily, the show was my scapegoat when Ahmed would ask me, "What's wrong now?" It was during a repeat episode that I got a phone call that changed the plan once again.

It was from one of my colleagues who worked at the consulting firm. He was calling to ask for my opinion regarding a contract position that he was recently offered. Immediately, I knew he was talking about the very position that I was just fired from. I maintained my composure as he chatted on and on about his concerns since he had little experience in this area and asked what my thoughts were about it. I politely addressed his questions and even posed a few questions of my own regarding when he was offered the position, when he would tentatively start, and if the contract was through the consulting firm. I never let on that he was being offered my old job.

Lucky for me, he was more than happy to reveal all the details, which I wrote down on the back of a bill envelope. I was too frazzled and upset to even be bothered with finding a regular piece of paper. I wished him luck and told him to feel free to contact me if he had any further questions or news about the position. The irony of this call was not lost on me. Later, I would be thankful that I had taken the initiative to document those important details. Being unemployed meant that my schedule was flexible enough to include some research, with regard to filing a formal complaint. I lodged the complaint the following day and within two weeks, I was notified that an investigation would be launched.

While I was basking in the glow and simple delights of my first trimester, I was also at war with my former employer. I was resentful that the awful experience was casting a shadow over the happiest time of my life. I mean, there I was being interrogated like a criminal in a felony trial, while trying to keep my stress levels from affecting my baby. I often felt like the prosecution was railroading me during the uncomfortably aggressive interviews. The back and forth verbal battles were ever-present as my belly grew bigger.

Midway through my third trimester, my proverbial trial was over and I had been found Not Guilty. My freedom was sweet like the cool breezes of summer air on a hot day. I felt relieved to be triumphant and exciting to be past this horrible experience. It was during that time that I found myself shifting into more and more of an unfamiliar body that seemed to be controlled from the inside out.

While my body was on autopilot, my mind required constant engagement from me. As I had suspended my job search until after I had the baby, I spent the majority of my time alone with my thoughts. Being acutely aware of everything was a full-time job it and of itself. I constantly worried about what type of parent I would be and if I even had the skills to be a good mother. I knew that parenting was a great responsibility and my concern was that I wasn't prepared for this undertaking.

My fears and insecurity kept me constantly reflecting on my childhood, as I evaluated my own relationships with my mother and father. Being a product of a teenage pregnancy, I carried with me an internal sense of inadequacy. I always had the feeling that I had robbed my mother of her potential life, so I developed a need to be perfect in order to make up for her loss. And having never met my natural father left me feeling rejected and abandoned. While my mother built a solid marriage with the man that I would forever call my father and who cared for me completely, there was always an underlying question of if I could truly be loved. What if my child didn't love me? What if I couldn't provide my child with the necessary love?

When I stroked my belly, I mindfully whispered the words, 'I love you' each and every time to build a habit of affirming and articulating my unconditional love. I reassured myself that the love I had for my mother and father, my siblings, my friends, and Ahmed prepared me to love this child.

The day before my due date, I awoke to a weird feeling that I wasn't quite able to pinpoint. These final months made eating to my satisfaction difficult, but I was determined that on this day I was going to have one of my favorite meals so I had a light breakfast and set out to do some laundry. By mid-afternoon, I had climbed my basement stairs 4-5 times and was a bit tired. I sat down and clicked on the television to watch Oprah. While chitchatting on the phone with my friend, she commented that I was making an odd noise every few minutes. I was totally unaware and asked her what she meant.

"You're making this *owww* sound. What are you doing?" she asked. "I'm just sitting here folding clothes and watching TV," I said. Just as she was about to respond, I made the sound.

"That that right there! What's that?" she urged.

"Oh that's just a little cramp I have, it's nothing." The 'little cramp' was actually the beginnings of my labor but I was totally unaware. My friend's concern grew and I assured her that I was fine and I had just seen my doctor a few days before. At my weekly appointment, I was informed that I was 100% effaced and that the baby could come any day now. I had joked with my OB/GYN that I was positive I would give birth on October 19th as I vividly remembered the night I conceived. Her retort was that she would be leaving the country that evening and that I should cross my legs until she got back.

So while I understood that I could possibly be in labor, I didn't put much stake in it and focused all my attention on my upcoming dinner. Once Ahmed arrived home, the 'little cramps' were occurring about every five minutes. His standard question of, "How you feel?" was met this time with, "I think I'm okay."

We debated for an hour and then finally agreed that we would go to the hospital and then to dinner. Months earlier, I performed a maternity tour and had the What-To-Do's down pat so this was simply a test run in my eyes. The exam was relatively quick and they confirmed that I was in fact in labor. I believed that the mild discomfort I was experiencing could be resolved with food, so I asked what were the recommended next steps hoping that it included eating.

A nurse advised that I simply go home and walk around a bit and return only when it became difficult to move. Upon leaving the hospital and crossing the parking lot, I abruptly stopped mid-stride and shook my head. Something strange had happened abruptly that stopped me in my tracks. To this day I can't put my finger on it. Ahmed spun around and before he could say anything, I told him that we could just go home.

In a split second it felt like a switch had been flipped. I felt a surge of energy that left me slightly lightheaded and I just wanted to go home and sit down. With night falling, Ahmed and I decided that we should go to bed. He had been at work all day and I was simply uncomfortable. Within minutes of getting into bed, I knew that I would not be able to lie down and didn't wish to disturb Ahmed who was now fast asleep. The house was dark and quiet as I wandered about looking for a comfortable place to rest. I remembered that the nurse had told me to return when I found it difficult to move and I believed that the time had come.

I climbed into bed and told Ahmed that I was ready to go to the hospital. I told him that I would wait for him downstairs since I needed a head start and was already dressed. Upon returning to the hospital, I was told that this time I would need to be monitored and within minutes, a nurse returned to hook me up. She asked me to lie back and I politely told her that I couldn't. As a lifelong asthmatic, I have difficulty lying on my back. As she pressed my shoulders towards the bed, I abruptly asked her to let me go. I could sense that I was a bit curt and apologized, but I couldn't bear to be touched.

Sensing that I wasn't going to cooperate, she left and came back with a pill. She told me that I needed to take it and shoved it into my mouth. Before I could ask what it was that I just took, she darted from the room and into the hallway where a group of people stood. It was several minutes later when she returned and told me that once again I should go home and walk around. I couldn't understand why I needed to go home, but I was agitated by her presence and I had no desire to continue talking to her.

Another nurse came into the room and unhooked me for the monitor and asked me how I was feeling. I responded that I was okay and asked about the commotion in the hallway. She said that another woman was in labor yet who wasn't due until February. As I slid myself off the bed, I walked over to Ahmed who was asleep in the chair. Brushing his arm, I told him we could go. It was 3:23 a.m. when we arrived back home. The late night air was chilly but felt good to me, as I was rather warm. Climbing stairs once again, I felt more uncomfortable and now needed to find a soothing spot to just sit down.

Ahmed headed up the stairs and back to our bedroom and I remained downstairs to muster up the strength to tackle yet another flight of stairs. By now, he knew not to dote over me too much. I'm like a hurt dog when I am in pain, I snap and snarl at everyone, even when they are trying to help me. As I reached the final steps, a rush of heat came over me and I felt as if I had been set on fire. I immediately stripped off all my clothes and headed to the bathroom.

I flung open the large bathroom window to catch the best breeze of my life! I inhaled deeply as the cool air hugged my naked body. In that breath, the discomfort subsided, yet I wasn't able to move so I flipped the toilet lid closed and sat down. I found myself slightly rocking back and forth and listening to my own breathing which as slow and deep. That delightful breeze continued to float in and out to the rhythm of my sways. Then a knowing voice came out of the darkness and instructed me to push.

Although there was no one there, this voice was audible to me, but I wasn't afraid. Obediently, I placed my left foot against the side of the tub for leverage and leaned forward. With that first push, my water broke and sprinkled my face as I blinked away droplets. I looked down and I saw two eyes staring directly at me. A smile crossed my lips and I leaned back to gaze on that little face. With every ounce of discomfort gone, I let out a breathy sigh of relief. But now, I had some work to do. With her head and shoulders out, I expected her to start wailing, but she didn't. In fact she didn't cry at all throughout the entire experience. At that point, I called to Ahmed for further assistance. As he crossed the threshold of the bathroom, I could see his analytical mind kick into gear.

"Oh, you okay?" he asked, in a very calm voice. But his eyes told me he was in shock. Hearing his voice, our daughter immediately began to turn her body in his direction, wiggling and arching. This child moved with purpose before she was even completely out of my womb. Startled. I hastily asked him to come to me. Looking down at our daughter, Ahmed and I marveled at her adorable face. "She has my nose and my eyebrows, and my lips," he said. The uncanny resemblance made me smile and his wonder touched my heart.

I had expected a messy delivery, but because the baby came out as my water broke, she was perfectly clean. As I reached for Ahmed, I felt yet another urge to push, and with him in front of me posed in an umpire stance I gave a final push, and Araina (a-ray-na) Kristina was born. Yes, gave her the name that her father had chosen for her when he was a child himself.

An indescribable joy touched in my spirit as I lovingly stared at them, cooing at each other. Cradling her in his arms, I watched as they exchanged glances and kisses. "This is love", I thought to myself and my heart was so full that all I could do was marvel at the two of them. As Ahmed turned and began to walk out of the bathroom, I quickly snapped out of the love haze and reminded him that she and I were still connected. He stared down at the now outstretched umbilical cord and frowned his face.

Once again I knew that Mr. Fix-it was hatching a plan, but I simply wanted to hold my baby. He placed her in my arms and she immediately began popping her lips. I touched her chubby cheek and nestled her onto my left breast. While she was a replica of her daddy, with an appetite. Stunned by the intensity of the suction, I grabbed a hold of the sink to steady myself. I could hear Ahmed moving through the house and muttering, but was unclear as to what he was doing. As he barreled up the stairs, he returned with a camera and started taking pictures.

I laughed and jokingly told him that no one wanted to see all this! I then asked if he had called the paramedics to which he confirmed that they were on their way. I could barely keep my eyes off of Araina. The little fingers, little toes, and little Buddha belly – everything was just exquisite. Marveling at every detail, I didn't even hear the EMTs arrive. Four large men hovered in my bathroom doorway and asked me if I am okay. Under the pressure of my quick dagger-like stares, they immediately lowered their voices to a whisper. "I'm fine, gentlemen," to which they began to explain what was to happen next. As they handed the scissors to Ahmed, one of the EMTs slowly told me that they would take me to the hospital. I shake my head to acknowledge that I understand and then I stood up.

Completely naked and cord dangling, I proceeded to tell them that they were *not* permitted to touch my baby and I would be watching them while I got dressed. They retorted, "Yes ma'am," in unison and stepped aside as I handed Araina to Ahmed to exit the bathroom. Everyone including Ahmed followed orders as though I was a seasoned drill sergeant. The ambulance ride was quick and I looked around to see where we were. I then asked, "Where are we?"

"We're at the hospital, ma'am," one of the EMTs replied as if he were speaking to a 2nd grader.

"I had a baby, not a lobotomy! What hospital?" I said gruffly. I was unaware that they had taken me to the closest hospital, which was not the same as the one I had previously visited twice that night. Shaking his head, Ahmed assisted me out of the ambulance and helped me up onto the gurney. With eyes glued to my baby, I watched as the EMT handed Araina to a nurse who wrapped her in a large white blanket. As we were whisked down a hall, I had to constantly reposition myself to see what they were doing to her.

A doctor reassured me that she would be fine and that they were checking her vitals and temperature. "She's 8 lbs even ounces!" a nurse called out. All I could see were Araina's tiny feet amongst the huddle of nurses. The doctor placed his face into my view and told me that now I would need to push. Still distracted with trying to see Araina, I hastily told the doctor I was okay. He said, "Yes ma'am I know but you need to pass your afterbirth. We can assist you if you need us to," and he placed his hands on my stomach.

Grabbing his hands forcefully, I rallied up a small portion of politeness to say loudly, "I'm okay!" I labored for several more minutes and breathed a heavy sigh when I was done. A nurse then came to take my blood pressure. I asked her when I could see my baby and the doctor answered, "Oh, she's under 24 hour observation. You can see her in a few hours." With a pat on my leg, he then said that I could go home.

I instantly sat up and asked him to repeat himself. He reiterated that I was fine to be released, yet I could not see my baby for several more hours and I would be unable to take her home. I have heard of people having outer body experiences, yet could not say that I fully put stake in those stories until that moment. I watched myself jump off the table and stand directly in front of the doctor. I heard myself say, "If you are going to observe her, I'll need to observe you observing her."

I listened as he said that they were under no obligation to keep me because I didn't have her there, however they were responsible for her first 24 hours of care. I concluded by telling him that there was no way I would be leaving the premises without my child and that I would require a room. And with that, I was assisted back onto the bed and wheeled to a room where I slept for exactly three hours with Ahmed by my side before buzzing the nurse to bring me our child.

A knock on the door made my heart leap as I eagerly anticipated seeing that little face, but I was disappointed when a young woman stepped into the room and told me that she would need some information. She was with Vital Statistics and told me that she preparing Araina's birth certificate. "Place of Birth?" she asked cheerfully. "At home", I said. "Attending Physician?" I glanced at her awkwardly as I had just told her that I had had my child at home. "There was no physician present," was the most polite response I could think of. "Oh, well we have to put someone's name down", she replied.

Dumbfounded, I looked at Ahmed and then back at her. "Well there was no one there but us." "Okay", she said and proceeded with some additional questions. As she prepared to leave, a nurse pushed open the door with transparent bassinet. I sat straight up and leaned over to catch an anxious glimpse of Araina. She was wide-awake just as she had been when I had her, looking around curiously. The nurse scooped her up with an array of blankets and handed her to me. My breath caught as I felt the softness of the blankets brush against my arms. Here she was this chubby little baby that I had to love and care for.

The hopelessness I had experienced when I initially found out I was pregnant had transformed into an endless ocean of hope that I wanted to dive into. I knew that fear would always accompany me on this journey, but I only had to stare into those big, brown eyes to be fearless.

*   *   *

As we prepared to leave the hospital, I dressed Araina in a matching white Winnie the Pooh onesie and cap. After Ahmed gently bundled her into the car seat. It was a rainy Sunday morning yet my contentment beamed through me like noon day sunrays. I peered into the backseat as Ahmed strapped her in securely. As he ran around to the driver's side of the car, I watched him through the rearview mirror until he plopped into the seat.

"We did it!" he said with an accomplished smile on his face.

"Yes we did." Uttering those words affirmed that all the pain, fear, and anxiety had been faced and now a new journey would begin.

When I think of the fact this started as an unplanned pregnancy, followed being unfairly fired, this had the potential to be an awful situation. But it turned out to be wonderful! From that point forward, I had a renewed spirit and a consuming love that would forever remind me that walking through fire yields fortitude. Over the years, friends have family started to call my daughter "Rain," short for Araina, which is ironic, because she the pure sunshine of my life.

7

Playing Small: Life Lessons In Self Doubt

MALLA HARIDAT

• •

"There is no passion to be found playing small - in settling for a life that is less than the one you are capable of living."
- Nelson Mandela

I wanted to be an entrepreneur at a young age. Even before I knew there was a word to describe the concept. I used to "direct" mock stage plays on the playground in school. I convinced friends to memorize their lines during lunchtime by reminding them how wonderful the applause would be. And my first attempts at marketing were posting flyers to spread the word and gather an audience. I look back at those experiences and realize the seeds for running my own business were planted during this stage. I wanted to inspire others to lead a big life. I wanted to be in control of my vision and my future. I wanted to work with a team who could inspire others to engage on a larger level than I had imagined.

I can also trace my entrepreneurial roots back to watching the daily struggles of my mother. She was a single mom who worked as a nurse on the night shift. Sure, it left her day open to shuttle me around to school and extra-curricular activities, but it had its limits. She often burned the candle at both ends by working double shifts while taking care of me. While she had support from family and friends, she was the main person responsible for raising me. It hurt sometimes watching her make the choice to take on an extra double shift so she could pay the bills. I knew I wanted something different for myself, something that required less sacrifice and would allow me to still be present with my family.

I reconnected with those desires when my own daughter was born a few years ago. I wanted to be there for her school plays, the daily hustle and bustle of prepping school lunches and school drop-offs. I wanted to have energy to help her out with homework instead of passing out after a long day at the 9-to-5 grind. Most of all, I wanted to be her role model. I wanted her to know that she could dream and be anything. All she needed was hard work, determination, mentors and a bit of grace along with God given talents. I held that dream when she was born and knew that I could show her best if I was living my life from that space.

The desire to be an entrepreneur who serves is wired into my being. My struggle, however is that I often shirk from reaching my full potential. I am on the road to recovery from the disease of "playing small" in spite of the fact that I don't work "small." I've received honors and awards that demonstrate to me that my work is not small. I can recall the New York Times feature article about my business, as well as placing first in a competitive grant competition for small business owners in New York City. I was also a finalist in a regional women's business pitch competition. Not to mention the numerous letters of thanks from students about my programs describing how my teaching changed their lives.

Then there is the positive feedback I've received from clients which emphasizes that I don't play small when delivering value to them. I don't mean to brag, but I know my work is solid. And yet, I have played quite small when it comes to growing my business. It is contrary to what I have done for others or trained them to do for themselves.

I have run from applause and hearing my name being highlighted even though I know that public accolades are key for business growth. When I've been tapped on the shoulder or given ideas of how to play bigger with my business, I have come up with excuses for why I can't move forward or found ways to stay under the radar and remain a best kept secret. Do you see a pattern here?

So I'm sure you're asking the questions that I often ask myself...what is stopping me? Why won't I play bigger? Why don't I take a more active stance when it comes to marketing, promoting and publicizing my message so that more lives are changed? I am certainly qualified, so why have I spent years not living up to that level in my life?

Here is a theory about where this pattern started, because I didn't always play small. And while I wish I could think of one pivotal event that caused the spiral, I believe it was a series of events over time. Each experience was responsible for crafting my skills, ideas and even the way I viewed myself.

Let me take you back to a stage in my life when I didn't think small. I started my first business at age 17 with only a belief in the possibilities. And whether it was my naive youthful optimism or a total lack of knowledge about all the things that could go wrong, I didn't approach the situation from a place of fear. So my first endeavor was a vending machine company that I thought would change my life.

I was emptying the garbage in my house one day and came across a flyer inviting people to come out to an event and learn how they could earn thousands by owning vending machines. These were not your grandmother's machines. They were smaller with only a few mechanical parts that were simple to fix. They were perfect for small and mid-sized companies to house in their lunch rooms. The size and lack of electronics on the machine made it accessible for anyone without technical know-how to run this business.

I begged a friend to attend the event with me. He was uninterested at first, but reluctantly attended. As the presentation loomed forward, even he was excited by the promises that the company offered. According to the presenter, I could refill the machines weekly/bi-weekly and earn the same amount as a typical college student while working in half of the time. Plus, I could even invest in more machines and earn double and triple my initial investment if I played my cards right.

As an adult, I understand that these seminars are mainly hype. But to a 17 year old young girl who was headed off to college and stressed over how she was going to pay the bills - it was like the heavens parted and God answered my prayers.

At first, I wasn't sure how I would get the money to purchase even one machine. My family wasn't rich; we were an average blue collar family living in the middle class suburbs. While I never wanted for anything, I also knew what it was like to wear hand-me downs and could make a mean lunch out of left-overs. We took family vacations which often consisted of road trips and overnight stays at lower priced hotels or the homes of friends and family. To this day, I always travel with a snack in my bag, because I knew better than to ask for a meal when we were miles away from low priced options.

Thankfully, fate was on my side. My grandmother, the family matriarch, passed a few months prior. And unbeknownst to me, she left me her car, a used Chrysler LeBaron. When I shared my dream with my mother, she offered me the ultimate option. I could keep the car or sell it and use the proceeds to buy the vending machines.

Of course, I choose the machines. Not your typical 17 year old decision. But I was so focused on my future and figured I could always buy a car another time.

I remember the day that the delivery truck pulled up to the house. I ran out the house in my pajamas and slippers not even caring that my cereal was getting mushy. I was on my way to being an entrepreneur! The delivery person helped us load the six machines into the garage. I tore open the business owners' box to learn more about how I would get the machines placed and all of the technical details I needed to get started. The company promised that they would help us get all of the machines placed. So, I wanted to roll up my sleeves and do my part to get started.

What I didn't realize is that placement meant sending me a box of 5,000 mailing labels and direct mailers. I bought stamps with money I had saved from working my fast food job and dropped the mailers off to my future happy customers - business owners who wanted more productive employees with fewer outside snack breaks. Then I waited for the calls to roll in. But a few days later, no one called. I was devastated. Those flyers looked so compelling. I just knew we would have all of the machines placed within a week.

A month passed and there was still no movement. I tried calling the company, of course they were no help. They offered to sell me another set of labels or references for a telemarketing company. I was all out of money and didn't think that a new list of mailing labels or expensive telemarketers who couldn't guarantee placement was the answer. Instead, I thought I'd wait for a miracle.

Now, my mother had other ideas. After the machines sat stationary for two months, she laid down an ultimatum. Get the machines out of the house or "else". And I knew my mother was serious about the "or else." So I threw on some dress clothes and headed out the door.

Except, I wasn't sure what to do. I didn't know how I was going to find good locations if the company I bought the machines from couldn't help me. There was no rich uncle who could make a few phone calls. I didn't have a ton of mentors who could help me negotiate the first placements. So I started knocking on doors in a business district close to my house and prayed that someone would say yes.

There I was, an inexperienced door-to-door saleswoman trying to earn my keep. Thank goodness I had hours of selling Girl Scout cookies under my belt. Of course, this sales process was completely different. I had to convince businesses to place these machines in their companies with the only perceived benefit that their employees wouldn't be as inclined to leave for snack breaks. It was a tough sell. I heard a ton of "nos." But I also heard enough "yeses" that allowed me to accomplish my goal. To my surprise, I placed all six machines in under a month.

It would be more than 20 years before I would take that kind of risk again. I lived most of my early adult life lacking the courage to take these bold steps and ask for what I wanted directly. I started listening more to other people's ideas and their fears about what could happen if I stepped outside of the box. I stopped trusting my instincts. Even when my mother gave me the ultimatum, I remember hearing a voice inside of me telling me that I could do this. As I moved forward, I started depending on other people's opinions and their logic of why something would or would not work.

I started living a life of playing small.

I can remember the first time that seed was planted. I was meeting with my guidance counselor in the early part of my senior year of high school. She wanted to see the list of colleges that I was applying to. In the pre-internet days, I researched my list by combing through books at the library and sitting on the floor of Barnes and Noble for hours. My Mother and I visited a few area campuses to get a taste of the college experience. I also spoke to as many college graduates that I could find trying to get ideas for what schools would be a good fit for my background and interests.

So, I was pretty proud of my list. I thought I' researched well. I knew I had a strong academic record and extracurricular interests, so I wasn't afraid to apply for top tier schools. But my guidance counselor took one look at my list and told me that all of the schools, except one local school, were a stretch. I was stunned. No one had ever told me "no" when I was going after my dreams. I usually either had support or a clear message that I needed to figure it out on my own. But no one blocked my path and told me there was no use trying. I spent my four years not fitting into the mold of what was expected from most of the Black students, and guidance counselor. I heard the voice inside convincing me that I had studied hard for years for this one moment, so I applied to my list of schools.

Getting accepted into a college that prided itself in academic rigor and a diverse student body was going to be a learning curve for me. I was definitely concerned about how much it was going to cost and if the price tag would be worth it. While my friends and family would be supportive, it was mainly on me to navigate the unknown next steps. I was extremely proud when I got acceptance letters to most of the schools I applied to.

But now, I had a new voice in my head when it came to making big decisions. I heard the voice of doubt....of potential failure if I were to venture too far outside of my comfort zone. I heard the voice whispering, "You shouldn't even try." Those voice haunted me for years when I would consider whether or not I should pursue opportunities.

The voice became louder when I stepped into the next phase of my life which was college. On the surface, I appeared to be on the fast track. I was attending an Ivy League college - the first in my family to do so. I landed solid internship opportunities and sought to take advantage of experiences that my new environment had to offer like hearing high profile speakers on campus or off campus events and conferences.

There was something else under the surface going on. And it was very subtle. When I shared concerns with friends and family about not living up to my potential, they just laughed at me because it seemed like I had so much was in my favor. But they were not present during my daily experiences when I watched myself choose the experience with the least amount of risk attached. It was a carefully well-crafted space of playing small.

I knew there would be an academic transition, only I didn't realize how far I would be stretched when I arrived on campus with some of the nation's brightest faculty and students. The summer before my first year, I spent weeks reading and taking notes on the required reading book, Homer's *The Iliad*. I had read books by Shakespeare and Mark Twain in high school, but this one was another level. I diligently summarized the story and made notes about the characters as my high school teachers had taught me and thought I was prepared for my first day of class.

On the first day, the professor gave us the syllabus which included several books I had never heard of. Yet, I wasn't concerned. I figured with some hard work and a few nights of burning the midnight oil that I could complete the readings.

It was when he started diving into the class discussion that I could see Dorothy wasn't Kansas anymore (I was Dorothy by the way). He started asking questions about the book, I mean deep penetrating questions where he pulled several quotes from the text and we spent half of the class discussing those lines and the theories behind the author's writing. Now, I was more accustomed to summarizing my thoughts, not dissecting the author's thoughts. Some students dove right into the discussion. They compared the book to other Greek stories that I hadn't read. Other students related the three lines to other sections of the book and what the author's intended meaning might have been.

To my utter shock and amazement, as my classmates shared their opinions openly, a few even disagreed with the professor about various points he made. And it seemed that the professor was encouraging that manner of opinionated discussion and asked for more examples. I found myself making mental notes to myself like: 1. Read and **memorize** every line of the text for the next class; 2. Read **every** book in Western civilization before you come to class; 3. Disagree with the professor for bonus credits.

Needless to say, this approach was completely foreign to me, especially being openly opinionated. I was raised and educated in environments where you did not question adults. At least not in public. I had to *learn* to challenge an idea and to present solid reasoning or data for that challenge in order for my opinion to be considered as a possibility. Of course, my ideas would be challenged by another student doing the same thing. But as long as I could back it up, it would be weighed on the same level of importance as even the faculty member who had years of research under their belt. This turned out to be a key part of the learning process.

It took me three and a half years to adjust this new style of learning. I couldn't just work harder to get good grades, which is what had always worked for me. I had to shift my entire way of thinking. For the first time in my life, I had a very hard time with school. And while my family and friends were sympathetic, they didn't have solutions. I cried myself to sleep with books in my bed on many nights - even after talking with third and fourth year students or visiting professors during office hours. I reached a point of physical and mental exhaustion with this new style of learning.

This shift showed up in other areas of my life. Previously, I had always been outgoing - joining clubs or volunteering to lead projects. But now, I was barely treading water. I didn't want to engage in too many activities and lose valuable study time. I had my free time reserved for stalking my professors in office hours or the grad students in the writing center and catching up on sleep. I did have a close circle of friends but, I couldn't volunteer to start new groups or lead clubs with the same vigor I did in high school.

I think this might be a pivotal stage in my life when my risk taking slowed down. I stopped thinking big and stayed in a narrow space of comfort. I found a tutoring job close to campus with a student struggling in math. I started working with him and really enjoyed it. When I told a few family members about this discovery, they referred several new students for me to tutor. I quickly stopped taking on students as I felt they were sending too many and I couldn't figure out how to handle more than a few students. A few years earlier, I would have jumped in and gotten help along the way. I had officially reached a point where I couldn't think big anymore, so I retreated and turned down the opportunity to grow.

I look back today and see the tutoring agencies that started up and grew exponentially during this time. All I can do is just shake my head at myself, thinking that I could have been a pioneer in that industry.

It wasn't as though I didn't take ANY risks. I was influenced somewhat by my peers who thought big and made big moves in their lives. I did step outside of comfort zones on numerous occasions, trying experiences that were completely foreign to me. It did require a great deal of preparation and calculations about how to navigate those steps. For example, I remember the first professional networking event I attended. I only went because a good friend coached me thoroughly on what to expect. She prepped me on collecting business cards, rehearsed my opening pitch, and helped me choose an outfit. Initially I wasn't going to attend because I thought I needed to study. Then she emphasized the importance of building a network alongside getting good grades. So I heeded her advice and wore my sharpest business suit to attend.

Now, you might think that solid preparation is a good thing, and it is. There is also such a thing as being over-prepared and not allowing yourself to experience the moment. I definitely fell victim to the latter. I would over-analyze and over-think every situation. Eventually, I talked myself right out of it. I lost the comfort level of stepping into new environments and figuring it out along the way. In order to feel comfortable, I needed someone to advocate for me or complete a high degree of over-preparation. If I didn't have that comfort level, I wasn't willing to apply.

Rediscovering My 17-year-old Self

I will be eternally grateful for all of the lessons learned and experiences I had in college. It opened up doors that were beyond my wildest dreams. The hard skills I gained by operating in excellence in professional environments can't be matched. After you write your first 50 page paper that is heavily researched, edited and reviewed by your class for a healthy discussion and debate, other projects don't seem as daunting. I had these experiences and so many others that prepared me well for high achieving professional environments.

The experience did come at a price to my personal confidence. I created a space with a narrow comfort zone and rarely strayed beyond the walls because I wasn't sure if I could compete at the same level - even though I proved on many occasions that I could. Rather, I felt the need to over prepare to ensure that I could play out in my mind every possible scenario and figure out how I would handle every outcome. If the end result was too risky or could lead to negative repercussions, I would opt not to play. The outspoken girl who used to raise her hand easily shifted into a reserved young woman who only raised her hand when she knew she could nail the answer and tackle the debate. The girl who knocked on doors willing to take a risk stopped knocking and kept her tutoring and other experiences small and limited.

The trend of playing small continued after college. I taught programs that educated young people on starting their own businesses. The work was revolutionary. We were changing young people's lives and teaching them how to fish - rather than waiting for the fish to be served to them. We taught concepts like business planning, goal setting, marketing, and techniques used to analyze Strength, Weakness, Opportunities and Threats (SWOT), to middle and high school students who often had limited exposure to business.

To an outsider, it might appear that I was playing big. I would challenge my students to actualize their ideas and number crunch their dreams. Students couldn't leave their ideas in the dream stage in my class; they had to make them real. Want to start your own fashion company but don't have the financial resources? Let's produce a fashion show with donated apparel so you can start networking in your industry. Thinking about opening a restaurant? Manage a catering event with your peers and to valuable experience, plus feedback from a group who will not allow you to make mistakes. In the days of before Google and The Lean Start-up, I helped my students create magic with their talents by learning to use a business mindset.

But while I was focusing on improving young people's lives, I downplayed my own value. The programs naturally generated press. It is the coolest thing to see a group of kids present a business plan or share a pitch about the type of company they want to start. When someone asked to interview me, I always found a way to avoid it. I would have someone else tell the story. I would refer the press to my students, parents or instructors. Mind you, I didn't have a fear of speaking up or speaking in public. I could teach a room full of high school students who are not afraid to show if they were bored. I didn't get nervous talking to parents at orientations who tossed out tough questions. I could confront vendors who charged us too much or event venues who left my 50 kids standing out in the cold because they "accidentally" overbooked the event.

However, if the press turned their attention directly to my story and successes, I found the first door to exit stage left. I made it my mission to avoid the spotlight. I didn't feel comfortable playing big because I didn't want to feel stupid and have people figure out that I wasn't as smart as they thought. Every day I watched entrepreneurs, business people, funders, and others making moves talk about how great they were. How great the kids were. How great the programs were. And I didn't have enough "swagga" to step back and see how great I was.

I didn't want anyone to compare me and say "well who does she think she is?" I just kept digging in to uncover the flaws rather than celebrating what I had achieved. I remember how vulnerable I felt one time in particular when I had to stand in the spotlight. It took everything inside of me to quiet the voices and ignore the fears. And in the end, I only found the courage because the project supported my students. Now I realize "who does she think she is," is the most powerful question ever when you put the emphasis on the right place.

These days, I can proudly say, that something in me has shifted and I won't allow myself to succumb to these disease of playing small. I can't tell you the exact day this thought really settled in my spirit, or the day that I started focusing on the opportunities more than the fears or voices telling me to stay in the comfort zone. But I started taking slow steps, and it's been the most humbling and rewarding journey ever.

My secret sauce has been challenging myself to take one step each week outside of my comfort zone. Small steps. Consistent steps. It's the continued commitment of these small consistent steps - akin to the process of how an athlete trains for a big event - that started reshaping the fears. It often scares the crap out of me, but each time I step, I gain new insights and courage to go forward. When it works and I win, I silence another voice that used to believe in the opinions of others were more valuable than my own. Each time the step doesn't lead to a win, I remind myself that I am having a learning experience. And it's all good. I remember to stay motivated to my dream that I came here to serve - rather than the former insecurities.

I can remember one of the first moves happened after the birth of my daughter. I launched the Mom & Daughters Inc., workshops after spending considerable time and resources rethinking my business model. After all of the years of creating custom programs for others, I had never created my own program. I thought about the concepts of entrepreneurship that weren't being addressed and brainstormed a workshop where mothers and daughters could learn about business, financial literacy and have a fun place to bond and connect with each other. I wanted a place where my daughter and mother could spend time with me and we would naturally learn and enjoy each other's company.

With my knees knocking, I launched my first Mom & Daughter Inc., workshop a few months after my daughter's birth. I left myself open to the possibility that if no one signed up in advance, I'd nix the idea and start over. I was humbled when 20 pairs of mother and daughter teams signed up to attend the event. People immediately got the concept. They gave me feedback on what they enjoyed and what needed shifting. It truly touched me that those teams came out to my event. Not some large brand that we all knew, but MY event. Most importantly, they shared that they gained something valuable from the experience.

Recently, I decided to share my story in this book. I'm a private person by nature and didn't think I had a story to tell. Sure, I share stories with my close friends and family. And I always give nuggets to my coaching clients or participants in my workshops, but I realized that I did have something valuable to share which was much more important than worrying about my former mistakes or limited thinking. I've gained tremendous insight into my story and hope it helps others on their journey. You can take a deeply ingrained pattern like playing small and shift it. You can play big in the world.

I'm focusing less on those voices that remind me to stay in the comfort zone and more on serving other entrepreneurs and entrepreneurs in the making who can relate to this story. It's a stumbling block, although it doesn't have to be a dead-end. Just a work in progress.

I encourage you to start taking your small step this week outside of your comfort zone. It's worth it!

Perfect Life, Perfect Mess, an Un-Perfect Tale

BRANDI STARR

* *

I am the example, the leader, the motivator, and in many cases...the mold. I am revered, respected, held in high regards. I am perceived as a go-getter, a risk taker, as fearless. And as preposterous as it sounds, I have even been believed to be super-human because things in my life just always go right. Many would say that I have lived the perfect life.

I grew up in a bubble of positivity. Raised in a middle-class neighborhood by a single mother who worked two jobs to put me through private school. I was my mother's miracle child and was therefore both spoiled and sheltered. It was not until I became an adult that I had any knowledge of the struggles my mother endured and the village that it took to raise me. I was always taught that I could be anything, achieve greatness, that there were no limits. My elders instructed me to be purposeful in my actions and always strive for excellence. I was not only encouraged but expected to live life at a higher standard. This pursuit of excellence is what shaped my years in high school and my life thereafter.

In my teen years, I was the president of this, and winner of that. I was always involved and excelling in school, my job, and extracurricular activities. My life was a set of social superlatives; most likely to succeed, most likely to follow the rules, most likely to run the world and the list goes on. By my junior year in high-school, I became acutely aware that people were always watching my actions and using me as the measuring stick to which others were held accountable.

For example, when preparing for a Summer Leadership trip, the business teacher was explaining to the group how to dress and carry ourselves professionally. At the event and I was her example. And by example I don't just mean referencing the way I handled myself. She went as far as showing several photos of me from past events and used them as a "what to pack" list for the team. In that moment I wasn't sure whether I should be proud to be the example or embarrassed for being a total teachers-pet.

Outwardly, I carried myself as though I did not care what people thought of me, but on the inside, public perception and expectations had begun to creep into my thought process. Typically, high school girls changed boyfriends more frequently than they changed lip gloss, and I was already aware of how promiscuity could affected a girl's reputation. That knowledge helped me frame my mind to stay with the same guy until after I graduated. Situations like those affected the way I made decisions.

I vividly recalled how I ended up moving to Atlanta. Just months before my 20th birthday I was on the phone venting to my mother about how much I hated Tallahassee. It was a one-horse town, and other than the colleges and government agencies, there was just nothing there. The Denny's even closed at 10 p.m. The last thing my mother said before hanging up was, "If you want to leave, go. Just pick somewhere and stay. You can't keep moving every six months."

I was confident, determined and not afraid to take risks. Within 4-hours of that conversation I decided to move, had secured a job, and plotted potential places to live. Some would call me insane for just packing up and moving to a city over 600 miles from home where I knew no one. But, I was eager to take on the adventure. Although my life had not been free of adversity my set-backs were always temporary and I always came out on top leaving me with nothing to fear.

My 20's were amazing and terrifying at the same time. The social pressures to overachieve were heavy. At that time, my focus was not on being happy or forging my own path in life, my goal everyday was to live up to my own hype. For instance, I was a store manager at a popular shoe store and one of the youngest managers in the South East Region. I exceeded my sales goals, and maintained a low loss prevention rating despite being in a high crime neighborhood. My store was consistently touted as the "Store to Beat."

Even with such success, behind closed doors I struggled with not being able to ask for help, fearful of being perceived as weak or undeserving of my job or accolades. There were managers in my area who were far more seasoned than me whom I looked up to and respected. I can remember sitting in my store before it opened, frustrated about things that I knew weren't being handled properly and picking up the phone to dial another store to ask for help. I hung up before anyone answered on the other end, fearing that if I opened up about where I lacked as a manager, they would look down on me.

Rather than asking for help, I failed to properly discipline my employees letting small issues morph into bigger ones because I wanted them to like me. I believed if they didn't like me they wouldn't work as hard as to be exceptional and that would, in turn, make me just average. And I couldn't be average at anything. As a result of wanting be liked more than respected, I ended up getting fired. My assistant manager was stealing cash from the deposit bags and leaving the bags in the safe for me to deposit the next morning. This created a paper trail that showed money was only missing from the deposits I made. Although my District Manager called me to his office and shared that he knew it wasn't me stealing, it was the fact that I failed to force my assistant to follow procedure. I was mortified, and in shock. I could not believe that I was being fired. I had to go back into the store to pick up my belongings escorted by a security guard!

My employees, who once looked up to me, looked on with sadness and disappointment in their eyes. I recall a few offering words of encouragement and others mouthing, "I'll miss you." Onlookers in the mall were pointing and whispering as I walked by. With my head literally hung down, I took the long walk of shame through the mall, escorted out by security.

During the same period, I was ending a relationship with my son's dad. We all have those relationships that we stayed in for way too long. Even though you know it's over, everyone has their own reason for staying. Mine lasted six years and was filled with enough drama and "He did WHAT?" situations that if I wrote a tell-all book, no one would believe it wasn't fiction. I'd like to chalk it up staying to being "young and dumb."

The reality is, I wanted my son to grow up with his father, because I didn't. Even though the embarrassment of the relationship was an easier pill for me to swallow, I didn't want to be judged for being a single mother and never married to my son's father. I'm thankful that we never walked down the aisle, but to this day it still stings just a tad to say that my son was not conceived within a loving marriage. I was raised with very traditional values and having a child out of wedlock is just something I was taught you didn't do. I still feel a bit of shame not having made different choices.

My mid-20's can be summarized as "Project X" (my parties were legendary) meets "Ferris Bueller's Day Off" (ditching work and responsibility with the same flair as the class-cutter extraordinaire) with a little mix of "Eyes Wide Shut" (a period of sexual and moral discovery). Looking back, this period in my life is where I was most ...me.

Being out of my tumultuous relationship gave me a sense of freedom that I had not felt in a very long time. For a couple of years, I think my sub-conscious went on vacation. The little voice in my head that kept me on the straight and narrow focused on living up to expectations was somewhere bound and gagged, trying to regain control .For a short period, I was free to just be me. I was a true socialite, the glue that connected so many people. Social media was in it's early stages of popularity and I totally owned my online presence. I lived my life online like a celebrity in my own little world, but without the real fame or fortune.

It was during this time that I met my husband Rod. To those that know us, the story of how I met my husband, how we became the best of friends, fell in love, and later married is nothing short of a fairytale. We met at a pool party during a time when we were both in other relationships, but our fun-loving, life of the party personalities allowed us to instantly bond as friends.

Throughout the first year of our friendship, he was in a long-term relationship. I was in and out of two relationships, going through a serial-dater phase. I referred to him as, just Rod. We were just friends and we wouldn't have had it any other way. That is, until things changed.

I can distinctly remember the first time I started to look at him differently. He walked into my birthday party in 2005 and I struggled to keep my cool. I felt flustered, bothered, and taken by surprise. He looked hot, the suit fit his slender frame in all the right ways. He smelled edible, his cologne was just strong enough that I could smell him in my presence. His energy was drawing me to him.

I found myself having to keep a safe distance because friends don't look at friends the way I looked at him that night. For the next few months the struggle was *very* real. I fought my feelings partially because I was afraid to ruin our friendship, but largely because I feared what people would think. When evaluating him against my perfect man checklist, he didn't have quite enough check marks in the must-have column and a few too many in the column of things he didn't do. In hindsight, when I look at all the things that truly matter, he is everything that I dreamed of and more. But at that time in my life, that list was everything. I wanted to walk around with a guy who had all of the things on my check-list on my arm.

What would happen if we dated and then it ended? After all, I was still recovering from the public embarrassment of my relationship with my son's father. How would I still be respected and looked up to if yet another relationship didn't work out? So for several months, I continued to fight against the feelings that continued to grow every time I even heard his name.

Rod and I's transition from being just friends, to being in a committed relationship was abrupt, unplanned, and the perfect next chapter in our fairytale love story. It was a Friday night, my best friend and I had a full night planned, but got bamboozled by some old dudes who thought getting us drunk in their hotel room was going to get them some cookie. The situation went from bad to worse when my best friend got sick. She was in bad shape and I was too drunk to drive, but staying in that room was not an option.

Rod was my knight in shining armor. He left the spot where he was, picked us up, drove me to tuck in my friend, then we decided to keep the party going at a nearby club. I honestly don't know how it happened, we still debate that night. Maybe it was the alcohol, or his glow from being my knight in shining armor. He says I kissed him, I say he kissed me, however, there is no debating that we ended up making out on the dance floor. He was such a great kisser, in that moment it felt like everything around us slowed down and the room began spinning.

I remember thinking, "Is this really happening?" and it was. At the end of the night, my brain regained control, rationalized all of the reasons why that could never happen again, and I blamed it on the alcohol. The next four weeks were more awkward than a 4th grade dance. We talked, but avoided talking about that night. We entertained the idea of there being an "us" and finally gave in and had our first official date.

If someone else were writing this story, they would describe the next two years as magical. We were the couple to be like, considered a perfect match, we made it look easy. So, it was no surprise when Rod planned a grand, very public proposal with friends and family coming from near and far to see him get down on one knee. I was completely surprised, swept up in the moment and the #CountdownToStarrdom, the moniker that we gave our wedding, was underway.

Being the center of our social circles, everyone we knew was invested in our impending nuptials. Wedding decisions were shared via social media and our wedding website, friends and family were busy making plans to travel to Atlanta. Pre-wedding, post-wedding, and day-after-wedding parties were being planned. It was a reality-tv-esque production without the cameras. We were planning the perfect wedding for everyone's perfect couple. It appeared that I had the perfect life, the perfect relationship, and a man perfect for me. When in fact it was a perfect mess, it was missing some very fundamental elements.

You see, I believe the five foundations of a healthy and thriving relationship are:

1. Laughter, if it's no fun, why bother?

2. Effective communication, which includes intimacy.

3. Boundaries and alignment, you have to be moving in the same direction, and playing by the same rules.

4. Emotional availability, both individuals must be open to, and prepared for, a relationship.

5. Trust, love is built on trust, and it is trust not love, that conquers all.

At the time that we got engaged, our relationship was only surviving while giving the illusion of thriving on laughter and love alone. From the beginning of our relationship, communication and intimacy were a challenge. We could talk for hours on end about everything and nothing, but struggled to have the conversations that really mattered.

His communication style is dominated by feelings, while mine is conquered by logic. He expressed his issues in a way that was colorful, animated, and passionate, almost to the point of seeming angry. My style of expressing my issues was accompanied by a supporting PowerPoint filled with examples and recommended resolutions. The lack of verbal communication, coupled with a medical issue that tanked my sex drive also lead to poor communication under the sheets. With both of us not feeling heard or understood, and an on again, off again sex life, we both shut down. I hid my feelings behind the word "fine" and he turned to others as an outlet.

During this time, I felt less than, not good enough, and like a fraud. Here I was this awesome communicator in all areas except my relationship. I had a history, a reputation of being this uber sexual being, yet I couldn't connect in that way in the only relationship that ever truly mattered.

His indiscretions hurt, they brought back memories of my ex who cheated on me the entire time we were together, often with people I called friends. To make matters worse, I don't think I ever really dealt with those emotions. Rod's choices brought about a lack of trust. Rather than deal with the issues themselves, my fear of being publicly humiliated by a man I loved again won out and I attempted to "handle him."

In my mind, if I could expose him, and show him how much his actions hurt me, he'd change, then the issues would somehow fix themselves. And I became *that* chick, the crazy girlfriend checking cell phones and Facebook messages analyzing the cell phone bill, cyber-strong-arming chicks who even looked like they might have wanted to step to him. My inner Scorpio was in complete control and although hidden well, my crazy was working overtime. I don't at all condone that behavior. Now, being an older, more mature woman, I recognize that if you feel the need to check-up on a man, the relationship is long over. But at that time it wasn't even about him, it was about self-preservation to keep myself from being embarrassed, again.

Over the years we had kinda worked through and moved past our issues, which largely consisted of sweeping things under the rug and choosing not dealing with them as the solution. In each new stage of our relationship, we'd get so caught up in the whirlwind of newness that we'd forget there was a big pile of mess that we had never dealt with.

Like most couples, we went through pre-marital counseling with the pastor who was going to marry us. Each week we'd meet at the pastor's home, sit around his dining room table and work through the scriptures and exercises. Counseling did, what counseling was intended to do. It identified the issues in the relationship that could put our marriage at risk. When concerns were raised or areas that we had never discussed were brought up, rather than give into the process and grow our relationship we lied...*lied* to the Pastor... a man of God.

I can't speak for why he lied, but for me, the #CountdownToSTARRdom was on. Our world was watching. We had money and our reputations invested in the wedding, and I could not even begin to wrap my mind around having to tell people that the wedding was off. Not to mention we had a beautifully blended family, how could we tear that apart? What if our friends felt like they had to take sides? How is that fair to them? I had nightmares about how people would react. I knew some would laugh, some would be disappointed, still I feared that some would even stop believing in love and marriage if we failed. We were the example, the couple to emulate, the friendship who turned to true love.

So as we sat in the pastor's house on the last day of pre-marital counseling, he asked us if after completing all of the counseling exercises whether we felt that we were ready to get married. There was a long pause. I contemplated speaking up, saying no, because there were far too many issues. I wanted to stay I still didn't trust him, that I was unsure if we could survive as a couple. I wanted to share with my soon-to-be husband, as well as the pastor that I was having second thoughts. I was questioning if friendship and love were enough when there were so many issues that had been unaddressed. Instead of saying any of that, I smiled, looked at Rod and lied. I affirmed I was ready. I lied about being confident in our marriage and its future. I looked into Rod's eyes and I knew that he knew I was lying and I knew that he felt the same uncertainty. But we both reassured the pastor that we were ready.

Because we were already living in sin by shacking up and having sex before marriage, the pastor strongly recommended that we not wait until February to get married. That we go before God as soon as possible, then have the public wedding that we planned. My stomach dropped. You know they say when you know better you do better, and I honestly hadn't given any thought in the past to the fact that our relationship was not pleasing to God. We reluctantly agreed, and set a date for the following week.

When we got in the car, what we should have talked about was the fact that we weren't ready. We should have discussed the issues that we needed to work through along with the hurt and distrust that still lingered in our relationship. None of those words were uttered, we dove into talking about the wedding. The big one in February and how it would lose some of its luster if people knew that we were getting married in advance. So we made the decision to keep our September 16th nuptials a secret. Only us, the pastor and our tax accountant knew when I dawned that beautiful white dress and my God-father presented me to Rod, that I was already Mrs. Starr.

The first couple years of our marriage were rough, past hurts and unresolved issues resurfaced, and we faced financial challenges. During counseling the pastor stressed the importance of guarding our marriage and not letting others in. Although what he meant was be cautious *who* you let into your marital issues, I used his words as my excuse to why I couldn't talk about our problems with anyone else. To compensate, I spent many nights crying my eyes out on the bathroom or closet floor because those were the places I could suffer alone without anyone hearing my uncontrollable sobbing.

On the outside, we maintained appearances and made marriage look easy. Although I loved him tremendously, I did not like him. I did not feel good about myself or our marriage. He had changed me; my marriage had changed me. Rather than just being myself, it was a constant battle of trying to be a good wife. I was trying to keep my mouth shut and not be combative...I was trying to always be respectful, even in situations where I didn't feel it was deserved...I was trying to behave the way I thought he wanted me to behave so much that I lost myself. I didn't really know what made me happy anymore; I didn't even know what made me...me.

I dreaded both our September and February anniversaries, I felt like I had made a mistake, twice. But how long did I have to stay before it was publicly acceptable to say I tried, yet it didn't work? I knew marriage was no cake walk, and I've heard many couples say that if you can make it through the first three years of marriage you are golden. So that became my benchmark and I drew my line in the sand. If things had not improved by the time we hit three years, I would walk away. I simply would deal with however people perceived me and my marriage after I got out and never looked back.

Then came the turning point. Because I had prepared myself to walk away if things didn't improve by my deadline, it also forced me to prepare mentally and emotionally for what would happen if we did divorce. I had to face how I would be viewed and treated if we divorced. And in forcing myself to deal with those feelings, came the recognition two things. First, that what other people thought about me or my marriage didn't matter. I knew tons of divorced people and did not think any less of them because their marriages didn't work out. Second, that I had to stop blaming Rod for all of our issues. Every time I pointed the finger at him there were four pointing back at me.

I asked myself what are *you* doing to improve the marriage? Playing the blame game was not helping me find out what my role was in this situation. I also started to question my *real* feelings as opposed to how the world thought I should feel. I questioned what my desired outcome was and not what outcome portrayed me in the best light. I allowed myself to be human, to not have to achieve at a higher level. I allowed myself to own how I felt, as well as the choices and mistakes I made. Instead of focusing on my problems, I focused on what I could do to change my situation. I no longer felt powerless and feared undesired outcomes.

*God grant me the serenity, to accept the things
I cannot change;*

*Courage to change the things I can; and wisdom to
know the difference.*

Living one day at a time;

Enjoying one moment at a time;

Accepting hardships as the pathway to peace;

*Taking, as He did, this sinful world as it is,
not as I would have it;*

Trusting that He will make all things right if I surrender to His Will; that I may be reasonably happy in this life and supremely happy with Him forever in the next.

Amen.

• • •

By our three year anniversary, our marriage had turned the corner. Trust was being rebuilt, communication was improving, I was beginning to enjoy being his wife again. And while things were not perfect, if such a marriage exists, I no longer felt like I made a mistake. In fact, I looked forward to our anniversary, it was a *take that* to all of the naysayers who were waiting on our marriage to fail; a *booyah* to my negative inner voice, and a *praise Him* to God because it was through prayer that I started to see my marriage, my husband, and myself differently.

As our marriage continued to strengthen, we decided we wanted to have a child together. Between us, we already had four pre-teens, but we wanted one of our own. We felt a baby would tie a nice bow onto what was shaping up to be a pretty awesome blended family. We actively tried for a while, then stopped. I never went back on birth control, so we shouldn't have been surprised when we found out that I was pregnant almost a year after we stopped trying. We were ecstatic, we only told a few of our closest friends and my mother, but it was difficult not to tell the world. We eagerly prepared for my seven week visit where we were going to hear our baby's heartbeat.

The doctor squirted the jelly on my belly and began moving the wand around. The more she wiggled the wand without finding the heartbeat the faster my own heart raced. Then she stopped, placed the wand on the counter and shared the news. There was no heartbeat, the pregnancy was not viable. She gave us a few minutes. I cried for a moment, got dressed, and we left. I fell back into old habits, I was 'fine.' I didn't want to talk about it. I didn't want to deal with it. We *were* having a baby then we weren't.

In the weeks following, I felt myself slipping into depression. I started buying into my own hype. How could this happen to ME? Things like this just don't happen to ME? How was I supposed to tell people that this horrible thing has happened to ME? What if they pitied me and start treating me different? What if my body is broken? Women were created to give life. Never mind that I had already birthed one child, what if I couldn't do it again? Now that my husband wants a child, will he leave me? These thoughts mixed with grief consumed me, all while the world watched believing I was at the top of my game.

You see, when I found out I was pregnant, I threw in an extra prayer that at least one of my friends would get pregnant too. How awesome would it be for besties to be preggo together, right? Not to mention our child would have someone to grow up with since our other children were older. Well God answered that prayer in a *big* way. For four months in a row one of my best girlfriends announced that she was expecting along with five others who were in our circle.

Populate the earth 2014 was in full bloom. And while I was thrilled that my friends were being blessed with children, it felt like I died a little bit inside with each pregnancy announcement. The experience brought Rod and I closer together, we both struggled with losing the baby. We even talked about trying again. But what if I had another miscarriage? I just couldn't.

It took almost a year before I could entertain the idea. Even then I had to be in control, as much as possible. I analyzed the calendar for every type of event that could affect us. Work commitments, social plans, holidays, birthdays, Super Bowl, every important date to our family was plotted on a calendar. I determined that January, February, or March were the ideal months to get pregnant. I tracked my ovulation alongside when we had sex, keeping "smiley face days" a secret as to not make sex a chore. Although I couldn't control the outcome, staying in control of the process was the only thing that got me through the fear of having another miscarriage.

I tried not to worry, but I was nervous the entire first trimester after conceiving again. Even after we heard the heartbeat the first time, I wanted them to check the heartbeat at every visit. Although I entertained social media for nine months with my #PreggoProblems looking back the pregnancy was textbook and fairly easy. We chose the name Parker as a unisex name and even livestreamed the gender reveal so that our family and friends could find out the sex at the same time that we did. My husband's children were all girls, so this was Mr. Starr's last chance for a biological boy.

As the technician began to type the gender on the screen my mom cried, and Rod threw his hands in the air and proudly exclaimed, "It's a penis!" There were no complications, no worries, and this time we were blessed with a beautiful baby, Parker Logan Starr.

I still struggle sometimes, more than I care to admit, with giving too much mindshare to how I am perceived and what people think, but I no longer let it control me. I've eased up on the pressure I put on myself to consistently over-achieve to focus more now on the things that make me happy and less on being the best.

There are two key things I learned along my journey:

- Live unapologetically and know that the only opinion of you that you should be concerned with is your own.

- Nobody's perfect, stop comparing your behind-the-scenes story with everyone else's highlight reel.

You only live once, live unapologetically!

"Life should not be a journey to the grave with the intention of arriving safely in a pretty and well preserved body, but rather to skid in broadside in a cloud of smoke, thoroughly used up, totally worn out, and loudly proclaiming "Wow! What a Ride!"

— *Hunter S. Thompson*

You are going to make mistakes, bad choices, and do things that aren't acceptable or are foolish to some. A lion never loses sleep over the opinions of sheep. Don't let other peoples' perceptions and opinions dictate your life. I am very thankful that my marriage has blossomed, I love my husband more than words can describe. Every day in some way, great or small, I'm learning to be a better wife. I could have wasted many of the prime years of my life miserable because I cared how other people perceived what was happening in my relationship and home.

I also think about the many missed opportunities I've had keeping up the appearance of a perfect life when in fact my tale is anything but perfect. For example, I grew up as an only child, but I have three half-siblings on my father's side. I could have had a better relationship with my little sister earlier in our lives if she didn't view me as some super-human that was somehow free from adversity. My business would have grown much faster if I didn't fear failing publicly. I would have severed ties with toxic people much sooner if I wasn't concerned with avoiding drama and gossip. The list goes on and on, I can't go back and change any of those situations. Instead, I can learn from them and not let fear, perception, or the opinions of others be a part of my journey.

If you know someone who appears to have it all together there is something you can take away from my story. No one is perfect and everyone has adversity, fear, and failures. Some just make it look easier than others and the ones who make life look easy are usually the ones struggling the most.

I recently saw an internet quote that read, "Stop comparing your behind-the-scenes story with everyone else's highlight reel." No matter how well you think you know someone, you only see a small part of who they are, the best parts of their life, their highlight reel. When it comes to your own life you are viewing the raw footage, you simply cannot compare the two.

9

When You Pray and The Gay Won't Go Away

BECKY A. DAVIS

. . . .

The Discovery

*M*y daughter was due home from school in two hours. She was 15 years old and in the ninth grade in high school. Her phone had been taken from her because she got in trouble. It was time for me to give her back the phone, so I went into my room to the place where I'd hidden it. I'd learned that when I was gone, my kids would come into my bedroom and use the phone and put it back. So I started hiding it.

I got her phone and put in on the table so that when she got home from school I could give it to her. Every time I walked by the phone sitting on the table, it was like the phone was calling out to me. I picked up the phone and began checking it to see who she was calling or texting and what they were talking about. As I began looking at her texts, I realized that there was someone that she liked. It was twelve years ago when I began to search through her phone and unlike today where you can check a text and see the entire conversation, you had to go to text messages to see who texted her and go to the incoming messages to see their reply.

I clearly knew she and the person she was texting liked each other. I kept reading to see if they had done more than text. I was searching to see if had had sex with who she was texting. Were they kissing or touching each other's body parts. I wanted to know. What I realized was that the person she was texting was another girl. I stopped and thought for a minute; maybe I didn't read that right. I went back to reading and it was a girl that she was in a conversation with.

I was shocked, and my heart dropped. I even don't remember breathing. I could not comprehend that my daughter was interested in girls. My mind immediately started to race. I began to ask so many questions to myself, like, "How did this happen," "Where did she get this from," "Why is she doing this."

I never had issues with gay people. I didn't treat them different, I treated them like anybody else. I had friends who were gay and I worked with people who were gay and had good relationships with gay people. No gay person could ever say, I treated them differently because I didn't. I felt like people had a right to their lives and I had a right to mine. I had my beliefs about the lifestyle based on my Christian belief and faith. As a Christian, being a homosexual, gay or lesbian was wrong.

When she finally walked through the door, I started up the usual conversation about how school was and if she had a good day. She answered and was getting ready to head up stairs when I stopped her. "Hey come talk to me for a minute," she came back and sat down.

"So who do you like at school this year?" I asked.

"No one really," she said looking at me.

"What about Sam, you don't like him anymore?"

"No, he's so immature."

"C'mon, tell me, I know you like someone," I probed.

"Nope!" She again answered, but I couldn't let it go.

"Jasmine, I know you like somebody, tell me." She gave me this curious look and she sat and thought for a minute. It was silent, which felt like hours but was for only a few seconds. Then she spoke.

"Why do you think I like someone?"

"I know you *have* to like someone at your age this is the time when crushes start." She paused another minute.

She knew I was asking because I knew something, she just didn't know what I knew.

"I like someone. You won't like it."

"How do you know I won't? I don't know who it is." She looked at me, with a look of being scared and she held her head down with her arms crossed resting on her lap. Her eyes slowly looked up. It was the same posture that our dog had when he was in trouble for tearing up something in the house. Then she finally she said it. The words came out of her mouth, and it felt like it was in slow motion as she spoke.

"It's a girl." I kept my cool because I didn't want her to close off talking. So I asked her more about it. Then I just got upset and began to yell and scream and fuss at her about it being wrong. I told her she had to end it and stop immediately. She said ok and walked into her room. I thought I had taken care of it. Boy was I wrong.

The Disapproval

I was so upset and hurt. The more we talked the angrier I got. She told me that it was just something people were doing and she would stop talking to girls. I was relieved. A couple of weeks later, I was washing clothes and went in her room to get laundry and realized that my husband's shorts were in her dirty clothes. I stood there thinking, "How did his shorts get in her basket?"

Jasmine came home and I asked her why were Will's shorts in her laundry basket. She made up some excuse and I let it go. Then it happened again, his pants were in her room. I had my suspicions so I asked her brother, who was one year younger than her, if she was changing clothes at school. He said yes. He said he would see her in the hall and she had on different clothes. I knew it, going to school in her clothes and changing into my husband's clothes once she got to school.

I didn't know how much I could take, it was enough that she was gay, but to find out she wanted to look like a man just wounded me. I sat in the floor and cried. I wanted the nightmare to be over. I am a girly girl and that was what I dreamed about for my daughter. I was grieving the death of my dream for my daughter.

So she not only was lying telling me it was a phase, yet she was dressing like a man. I was embarrassed. She went to school with a lot of friends who we went to church with. Then I began wondering how many people had seen her in those clothes and whether or not they told their parents. *What were their parents going to think about me and my husband?* I was ashamed of what she was doing. It was like she had no problem with what people thought, which angered me.

The truth of the matter was if she was girly gay, I would have been ok with it because no one could tell. I had even said, "God why can't she just look like a girl and be gay." My mind was going crazy. That's one of the reasons I knew it was me who had the issue. I began to pull away from her and our relationship was going down fast. The more I got angry, the more she would do. When she did normal teenage things, I made it about her being gay.

I felt guilty, feeling like I failed as a mother. Her father and I divorced when she was almost five and I thought that maybe that was why she did this because she always wanted her dad and I to get back together. My relationship with her changed from that point and continued in a downward spiral.

The Death

As I began to pull away, she began to distance herself from me. We had been in this nightmare for over six years. Our relationship had totally changed from the time I found out she was interested in girls. I use to hug her and hold her hand, but I started pulling away because I was mad at her.

She graduated from high school and I just wanted her gone. She moved to Nebraska where her dad lived and I was relieved because now people wouldn't know. I can live my life without people looking at my daughter or me crazy.

I was so focused on me, me, me, that I never took the time to ask her what was going on in your life or in her mind. I just wanted what I thought was a normal life. I would talk to my daughter to see how things were going in her life. We never talked about anything personal in her life. We discussed people in the family, her job or just light conversations. She didn't bring up anything and I did either.

I immediately missed Jasmine when she left. So much that I cried for weeks. She had never been gone from me for more than a summer to spend with her dad. It had been she and I for years. I wanted her to come home to visit, but she always had an excuse why she couldn't come.

I was missing my daughter. I hadn't seen her for two Christmas' and Thanksgivings. I'd talked to her on her birthdays, but a phone call was a far cry from a hug or a kiss on her birthday. I was longing for her presence. Jasmine was so funny and witty and I ached for that. She had always been a caregiver, anytime I didn't feel good she would go in the kitchen, make hot tea and bring it to me in bed. She'd been like that her whole life. I missed laughing with her.

Our personalities are so much alike, she could start a joke, I would finish it and we would crack up. I was missed that. Some mornings I went in her room and jump in the bed and kiss her all over her face, but she was gone and it didn't seem like she was coming home anytime soon. I knew our relationship was weak, sadly I didn't realize how weak until she refused to come home. I was losing my daughter and I hated the way it felt.

The Divine

I had been praying and asking God to fix my daughter and our relationship for six years. I was really getting discouraged. I was sitting reading the bible one day and came across, John 13:35, "By this shall all men know that ye are my disciples, if ye have love one to another." That scripture hit me in the gut. I was being a hypocrite, I felt. I read it again and again. I started crying because I realized that I could show love to everyone I came in contact with, I could give advice and minister to other people who were going through tough times, but in my own home my daughter had not felt the love of her mother.

I began to pray and it was the first time I asked God, "What are you teaching me in this situation?" The answer was so clear. I looked down at my bible and there was the answer, love.

I knew that I had withdrawn my love away from my daughter, thinking that if she felt me pull away she would stop liking women so our relationship could get stronger. I was basically trying to force her to choose me or be gay. I was hurt realizing she was not going to change for me. I began to continue reading the bible asking for more answers and read Ephesians 6:12, "For we wrestle not against flesh and blood, but against principalities, against powers, against the rulers of the darkness of this world, against spiritual wickedness in high places." I started to see things differently. I had been wrestling and fighting with Jasmine for years and the fight was not with her. Because I could see, feel and touch her, it was easier to fight with her instead of spiritual darkness. I thought I was trying to be a good Christian, however I was breaking the most important rule, the reason Jesus came to set us free, the reason He did for me, LOVE. I started thinking about all the things I had done wrong in my life, yet God forgave me and I was not forgiving my daughter. I felt like a Christian fraud.

At one of our church's monthly ladies bible class, I felt the need to be transparent and share what I had done, what I had felt and how I had not shown love to my daughter. I shared with the ladies that I was worried about what church people would say because churches can snub their noses at gay people.

I knew I had to fix my relationship with Jasmine. I asked God to forgive me for what I had done to Jasmine and I knew I needed to call her and ask her for forgiveness.

The Dialogue

My heart ached more and more for my daughter and God was really working on me. I was listening to a radio station and the topic of discussion was how many homeless kids were on the streets because their parents put them out. There were several youth calling in and sharing their stories. I could hear the hurt in their voice as they spoke about how their parents rejected them. Then one caller called in and said that their friend committed suicide. In that moment, all I could think about was, "what if Jasmine felt the way they did?" I thought to myself, *I'd rather have her alive and gay then dead and gone.*

At home reading my bible, Ephesians 4:32 jumped out at me. It reads, "Be kind to one another, tenderhearted, forgiving one another, as God in Christ forgave you." I knew I needed to forgive and stop holding back because I want to be forgiven for things I have done that were not pleasing to God. I knew I needed to make amends and talk to my daughter. I called Jasmine one day and told her that I needed to talk to her. My throat was dry, my stomach bubbled...I did not know if she would open back up to me.

I told her God had been working on me. He showed me who I was and what he showed me was that I was not keeping his commandment of love. I apologized to her for all the hurt I had caused her and as I spoke tears rolled down my face. I was so full of emotion.

* * *

She sat on the phone and just listened to me. I asked her to tell me some of the things I did that hurt her. She was reluctant at first, clearly not to do the same thing I had done to her. So I began by telling her things I knew I had done that were not right and I could hear a muffled cry on the phone. I heard her sniffle a couple of times and she was quiet, so I stopped talking to listen and she just keep sniffling. I asked her was she and okay and she said yes, and I could hear it in her voice. I waited for a minute and there was silence. Then she spoke and said, "I've always loved you Mom. I knew you always felt hurt and disappointed when I was around." She went on to say she stopped coming around because she could see the hurt in my face when I looked at her.

Jasmine told me that when we went places, I would act like I wasn't with her so people wouldn't know, and she further explained how much that hurt her. Then she paused and I could hear her crying. She said the one thing she remembers like it was yesterday was, one day I looked at her and said to her, "I wish I had never had you."

My heart hit the floor. My cries turned into a sob that I could not stop. In that moment, I felt like the most horrible mother in the world. As I held the phone, I closed my eyes and put my hands over my mouth and wept. Tears were hitting my desk so fast that when I opened my eyes, it looked like I spilled water on it. I did not remember ever saying it, but I didn't deny it because I was so angry with her in those days, I could have, and since it was the first thing she said, I must have.

What really upset me was it had been six years and I had put a burden an additional weight on her that she had been carrying around all those years because of me. That completely broke me. I apologized to her for ever having said that and told her how much I love and missed her. I told her that I know saying it was only a start. I had every intention of showing her and that I would live the rest of my life replacing the bad memories for the last six years with new ones of love. She accepted my apology, excitedly looking forward to renewing the relationship between us that she so desperately wanted.

From that day forward, I did what I needed to do to show my daughter love and to live as a loving Christian and not just a talking Christian. I flew her to Atlanta about six months later. I prayed and asked God for strength not to get upset when I saw her looking like a man. I picked her up from the airport, I hugged and kissed her all over her face. My daughter was at home. Finally home. We spent a week together.

When we went out in public, I held her hand because I use to do it before I found out she was gay. She looked at me and just smiled and I could see the look of love and how much it meant to her in her eyes. It's the look when a mother knows their child is happy. Her eyes said, "Thank you mommy." I didn't care what others thought anymore; I only wanted to please God. In the past I wouldn't want anyone to think I was gay being with her, so I would walk off. This renewed mommy, she felt it; my love for her and it was the beginning of healing our relationship.

Later on, trying to be more comfortable with her lifestyle, I asked her one day to tell me about who she was dating, and she just paused.

"What do you mean?"

"Tell me about your friend. I talk to the other girls about their relationship and can give them some input on relationships, but I haven't done it for you, so tell me about her." She took a minute and slowly began telling me about her girlfriend. It was another milestone in our relationship. That was clearly something she had been wanting to do, she began to tell me everything. She began to tell me that she wanted a baby and she wanted her girlfriend to get artificial insemination. She asked about my thoughts. I had no idea what direction her relationship was going since we had not talked about personal things.

I was there to talk to her about it and gave her the same advice I would give my other girls. At the end of that conversation she said to me, "Mom I've wanted to have these type of conversations with you for years." My heart was happy because I knew it meant something to her.

Six years had passed since we began the work on mending our relationship. I have the greatest relationship with my daughter now. She is one of the smartest people I know. She is such a comedian, she'll have you laughing all day. She looks like her father, but has the personality of her mother and I love it. I had overlooked all the great qualities about my daughter being focused on one aspect of her life.

There was a great deal that I learned about myself and my faith in Christ. I realized that while I was focused on Jasmine, God was focused on me. He loved me enough to show me who I was and it was not pleasing in his sight. The hardest thing to do is to look inward. It's easy to see the other person's wrong but not your own.

The lessons that I learned from this were:

1. You can't be a Christian and select what parts of the bible you want to adhere to.

2. Love is a healer of relationships.

3. We can love and disagree at the same time.

4. We can't be so holy as Christians that we snub our noses at homosexuals because Christ came for all of us.

5. If you are a Christian and don't show love to others, you are not a disciple of Christ because it goes against the scripture.

What I know for sure is that love heals. All of the hate that goes on in the world can be healed with love. If only we take the time to love through our disagreements. My relationship with my daughter had flat lined, but God gave it a heartbeat again. Love heals.

For Better or Worse, but Worse Comes First

T. RENEE SMITH

. . . .

My life's journey has not been a straight path. It was filled with bumps, bruises, minor collisions and major accidents. It wasn't always easy. I was faced with a lot of challenges, set-backs and defeats. However, it made me the person that I am today and I wouldn't change any of it. The majority of my 20's and early 30's was consumed with doing what everybody else wanted me to do, helping other people build their dreams, and living out the life that someone else had planned for me. Whether it was the friends I selected, the college I went to, or the first business I started, I was primarily living out the desires others had for me.

After being in a toxic relationship for more than 10 years, filing bankruptcy for one of my companies, being on the wrong side of the law, and losing almost every prized possession I owned including my house, cars, clothes, and jewelry, life hit rock bottom for me. For many years I was ashamed of my past, disappointed by the decisions I made and wished I could have a "do over" with my life. For years, I felt obligated to make amends with my family for the hardships that I had put them through. However, now I understand that what I went through was not just for me and was never meant to be kept a secret. God delivered me so that I could help other women live an authentic, prosperous and purposeful life.

The Fairytale Is Over

So, I may not be the type of person who you think of when you imagine someone with low self-esteem, major insecurities or being paralyzed by fear. Well, if I look back many years ago that was the person staring me in the mirror. I grew up middle class and had a good childhood. Both of my parents worked in education system. Since my mom was a teacher, she knew most of my teachers and had me on a pretty tight leash. I grew up a bit sheltered and very trusting. I was an A/B student, SGA (Student Government Association) President, participated in dance, drill team and did all of the things that were expected of me. I graduated with honors and went to the college that my parents wanted me to. I pledged the Delta Sigma Theta sorority, just like my mom expected and graduated college in three years. If I look back now I guess I was being taught to be a people pleaser at an early age.

At 19, I thought I'd met my knight in shining armor; he was seven years my senior. I was instantly smitten with him because he was very charming and knew all of the right words to say. In the beginning, I received dozens of roses at my house or internship, ate at 5-star restaurants, and shopped at stores that I could barely pronounce the name of, such as Emeraldo Zegna, Diane Von Furstenberg, Bvlgari.

We built several successful businesses together and enjoyed a life of luxury, including million dollar homes, expensive cars, exotic vacations, and designer clothes. Then one day, things changed. Unexpectedly, the phone rang at 2:00 am, and I was dethroned as queen; the fairytale was over. My boyfriend of over 10 years called me and told me that he had recently gotten married and his new wife of four months was expecting their first child.

What? Wife, married, child, are you serious? We were just together in New York that past weekend? I was trying to catch my breath so I would not hyperventilate, as I looked at the phone in total disbelief, not understanding any of the words that were coming out of his mouth.

I was in complete and utter shock! How could the man that I had built a life with over the last 10 years, or so I thought, do this to me? In my mind, we were headed to the altar soon and would start our own family.

He had already proposed to me very early in our relationship and I felt I was too young to be married, but I always thought in my heart we would be together. Our relationship was by no means perfect, yet I felt like we had worked so hard together in building a business and spent so much time together that the natural progression was marriage.

My heart was completely broken. This was in essence the only man I had ever really known. Sure, I had silly little crushes in high school, but nothing of real substance. He and I had lived together off and on and spent most of our time together since we met. Yes I was shacking and my parents were not proud of it, forgive me Lord. My life had completely revolved around him for so long, I had no idea of who I was without him. I alienated friends and family for our relationship so it was always he and I, Bonnie and Clyde.

During our relationship, my ex often discouraged me from spending a lot of time with my family or friends because he told me that he didn't feel like they liked him and weren't comfortable around them. It was almost like he gave me an ultimatum without saying it. Whenever I was with my family or friends he would call at least 8-10 times leading into an argument whenever I got back. I didn't enjoy myself when I was with them because of the pressure and the process was so exhausting for me. Most times I just chose to not even hang out with family or friends.

How am I supposed to deal with this new reality of not having him in my life because he was always the person that I shared everything with? He always gave me direction about what I needed to do and I had become dependent upon that. In retrospect, it was more of him telling me what I should be doing, more like a father figure versus two partners making a decision together. The seven year age gap showed up frequently in our relationship because he had expectations of me, being more mature than I truly was. I guess I had lost my way and the ability to make sound decisions for myself. This would turn out to be a huge downfall for me allowing someone else to determine the fate for my life.

My life spiraled out of control. I had alienated my family, endured mental and verbal abuse, and placed my life on hold so he could pursue his dreams. That may sound bad, but it gets worse. I supported, loved, and placed this man first in my life for more than a decade.

Fast forward a few months...I found myself on the wrong side of the law and I lost everything. The beginning of my 30's did not start off well. I was 30 years old and in the midst of personal heartache where I had to figure out how to dissolve the businesses my ex and I had built because I knew we could no longer work together. We still had several outstanding business lines of credit that we owed substantial amounts of money on and we had to figure out how to pay them off. There was one real estate property with some equity in it. I decided to take the equity out of the house and use it to help pay down some of the business expenses. I went to the attorney's office to sign the paperwork which should have only taken about 30 minutes. However, the events that took place during this day will forever change my life.

The attorney took me into the conference room and told me to have a seat and he would be right back. As I got comfortable in my chair, nine FBI agents storm into the room, verify who I am, and tell me I am under arrest. A female and male agent take me into a room and start to question me. They were polite, but definitely drilled me and wanted answers to their questions. This was so surreal! I was truly having an out of body experience. When this first happened, I was physically present, but my mind was somewhere trying to process everything that was going on.

I am sure they told me, but at that point, I had no idea what I was been charged for. Once I really came to, you would think that I was scared and nervous. For some strange reason I felt a peace and a calm. For so long I felt like I had been trapped in somebody else's body just looking at life from the outside. I had become numb to the disrespect, lies, verbal abuse, and subtle cheating; I couldn't prove it, I just knew in my gut something wasn't right. This was definitely not the life that I wanted for myself, but I would always say, "At least I know what I have in this man."

I didn't want to go back out and start dating, because I may get something worse. What kind of thinking was that? How low must my self-esteem have been? I wasn't angry or mad I was actually happy. I had been praying for a long time that God would deliver our relationship and make it better. I was praying that He would change my ex...that of course was the wrong prayer. God answered my prayer totally differently than I ever expected; he changed me and gave me an exit out of the relationship and business.

Because my state of mind was so messed up, if I had not been provided with an exit I would probably still be there today. I am a very loyal person when in a relationship. We are together, no matter what. However, I had to now defined my boundaries about how "what" was described.

After a few hours of questioning I was taken to a detention facility. It was late one Friday afternoon, so I spent the night in the facility and would have a bond hearing on Monday. When I walked into the Atlanta detention facility with a group of women, it was so late in the evening that everyone was getting prepared for lights out. I asked the guard for a bible then proceeded into my cell and sat on the top bunk.

What thoughts were going through my mind? Lord, am I really in prison? Was I just free a few hours ago and now my life has completely changed? Many more thoughts raced through my head until I finally got to, "Thank you, God that I am finally free of the mental prison I have been in for quite a bit of my adult life." Constantly feeling like I'm not good enough, walking on eggshells watching what I say because I don't want to set my ex off, being careful of how I speak to men so my ex doesn't think I'm cheating and so on.

After a long weekend in the detention facility, thankfully, the judge let me out on bond. Thursday of the same week I was sitting in the U.S. Attorney's General office explaining to them why many of the loans that our businesses obtained over the last few years were not all legitimate. On Thursday of the previous week, I was living in an 8,000 square foot house with a massive closet bursting at the seams with designer everything, and a 3-car garage that housed two Mercedes Benzes and a Hummer. The judge ordered me to not go back to the house and to leave all of my possessions there. Practically everything I owned was seized by the government and later sold at an auction. The day I was released I moved back into my parents' house with just a few clothes I had on my back. All of the material possessions were gone.

The world that I once knew was instantly gone. One day I had every material possession I thought I wanted and the next day, I didn't. It was such a humbling experience and showed me that truly the most valuable thing you have in life is your faith in God.

A lot of people think that once they get money it will solve all of their problems; I am here to tell you that this is not the case. For many years I had an abundance of material possessions, but I was broken on the inside, in an unhealthy relationship, stressed about business, not eating, walking in constant fear and always looking back over my shoulder. That was not a life of total prosperity. Total prosperity is when you are whole, peaceful and have joy in your mind, body and spirit. I realized that money is not the root of evil as so many people misquote the scripture; it is the love of money that is the root of all evil.

Money is neither good nor bad until you put it into a person's hand. Money amplifies who you are. If you are a giver, the more money you have, the more money you will give. If you are stingy and selfish, the more you have the more you will hoard. Money doesn't change the essence or character of who you are it reveals and amplifies it. If you look at Oprah for example, she is a teacher and giver at heart. The more money she has, the more she gives away and the more opportunities she has to use her platform to teach and inspire others.

In addition to adjusting to life back with my parents at 30 years old, I was placed on home confinement with an electronic bracelet. The next year would be filled with grueling with court dates, depositions and debriefings.

The Queen Meets Her King

My 30's sure didn't start out how I would have expected. My closest confidant was my attorney and the people I talked to most were my probation officer and the United States Attorney Office. There had to be a silver lining somewhere in my story. One Sunday, I was sitting in church listening to the pastor teach about the role of a husband and a wife. After service was over I looked to my left and saw a very handsome man name Anthony. He and I struck up a conversation and later exchanged numbers. After talking on the phone for weeks, we finally decided to go out on a date. We met at Red Lobster and had great conversation as I stuffed my face with cheddar biscuits...I just love them.

Our relationship moved fast as I started developing really serious feelings for Anthony. I knew that I had to tell him about my legal troubles. I wasn't sure if he was going to still want to continue to see me after finding out the truth. One day I sat him down and told him that I needed to discuss something serious with him. In his efforts to lighten the mood he said, "You aren't a man are you?" I said, "Of course not!" To which he responded, "You can tell me anything." We both laughed and joke and then I confessed.

I didn't bog him down with all of the nitty gritty details, but said just enough to give him an idea of what was going on. I said that I believed probation would be the worst of my sentence and then I could move forward, finally able to put the whole thing behind me. We developed a really strong bond and got engaged within four months of meeting, getting married within a year. Our courtship moved fast and our marriage moved even faster.

Just a few months after being married I found out I was pregnant. Anthony and I were both overjoyed and our families were elated. However, this joy was short lived. Remember the previous year I was going back and forth to court and was on pretrial probation. Well as fate would have it, just a few months after being married my court sentencing came up. I went to court prayed up and ready to hear the judge tell me I would receive probation for participating in obtaining fraudulent loans. However, the words that came from the judge literally shook me to the core.

"T. Renee' Smith, you are hereby sentenced to 46-months in a federal prison camp. You will be given time to get your affairs in order and will report within 60 days." My knees went limp and all I could here was my mother screaming in the courtroom, "Oh no, my baby!" I couldn't bear to turn and look at my husband. What in the world was he thinking? This should have been the happiest time in our lives. I was a newlywed, expecting our first child and excited about building our life together. Instead of basking in these joys, I was preparing myself to go and serve a 46-month prison sentence.

Needless to say the upcoming months were very stressful. I couldn't wrap my head around the fact that I was about to leave my family for several years. Well since this train was moving and not stopping I had to get prepared. On a side note, my ex-boyfriend received a sentence almost four times what I received.

My husband and I had a very candid conversation. I told him, "Honey, I know that this is not what you signed up for when we got married and I know that you have needs. Therefore, if you want to walk away now I completely understand." Anthony said something so profound to me that I will never forget. "Why would I make a permanent decision that would affect our marriage based on a temporary situation." I should have known right then and there the type of man that I had married.

216

And The Journey Begins

After being at the camp for several months, I was ready to give birth to my first son. I was induced and delivered a healthy 8 lbs. 5 oz. baby boy. I was able to stay with him in a program for 11 months. After that, my husband raised him for the next year and a half without me. The entire process of me being away was a test of strength, will, faith and endurance. It is not easy being separated from your family, especially being a newlywed and have a newborn.

During my entire three years in prison, even though the sentence was for 46 months I only served a portion of the time, I think I was in denial. I would always say that I was on vacation, an extended retreat, a bible college, some sort of excursion like that. I don't think I was actually dealing with the realities of the situation because it helped my time go by faster. I immersed myself in teaching, writing, learning and exercising. I did ghostwriting for two books, developed small business curriculums, and taught bible study. I was busy from the time I woke up to the time I went to bed.

That kind of activity was good in the sense because it kept my mind focused. It was bad in the sense that I wasn't dealing with my emotions. I didn't deal with anger, resentment, unforgiveness and a range of other emotions I was feeling. Therefore, many of the unresolved issues I had from my previous relationship were spilling over into my marriage. You would think that I would have been a very appreciative and loving wife because of my husband's support. Sometimes, I was, while other times I was emotionally unstable, selfish, and downright confused.

There were instances where my husband and I would have the most loving conversations of how much we missed each other and what we were going to do when I got home. Other times, not so much. I would ramble on and on about what was happening in my day, what I needed, and how I wanted things. Looking back, I wasn't sensitive to all the craziness my husband had going on in his life. He was working, raising our son and teenage daughter, from a previous marriage, while having to perform the roles of a mother and father in my absence. That's enough to stress anybody out.

I think the time away was so emotionally, mentally, and spiritually difficult for both of us. My husband was trying to maintain the home front, also bringing our kids to see me. He had help from my parents and brother, however, the bulk of the responsibility fell on him. I was so emotional because I would see him and the kids for a few hours in visitation and then be heartbroken because I couldn't go back home with them.

One way I protected myself was by becoming somewhat emotionally detached so it wouldn't hurt so badly. I would be physically present, but not 100% mentally and physically present. Behaving like that can catch up with you after a while and you can become desensitized. I know it had to be difficult for my husband to be primary caregiver over a two year old. All of the things that I would be working on with our son on such as potty training, learning to talk, and pretty much every skill needed were on my husband to perform. In addition to making sure that we were financially taken care off.

My husband and I both believed that me being pregnant and giving birth to our oldest son during this time was a blessing in disguise, as my father says, because for me I was so focused on my son during the first year that I didn't have time to concentrate on the harsh life I was living in prison. And for my husband, he was so focused on making sure we had everything we needed that he didn't have time to think about anything else.

The years went by and it was finally time for me to come home. Hallelujah and thank you Jesus! I was so excited about going home and being reunited with my family. When I first got home, my husband and I worked on gelling and finding our rhythm. It wasn't like we had lived together for a long time and really knew each other's ways before I left, so this was all very new. We had only been married a little over six months before I left. My husband had moved into a new house which meant I had to get comfortable in a new environment. I was rebonding with our son, our daughter had moved out by that time, learning his new personality and getting settled within a new career and business. Needless to say, it was a huge transition period, one that was filled with a lot of frustration, misunderstandings but a bunch of grace and love from my husband.

One of the hardest things that my husband had to deal with was my transition. I was often told that however long you were away that is how long it will take you to transition. Initially, I didn't believe that, but as I went through our marriage I found it be very valid. I was one person when I left and totally different when I came back. In some ways, I had been shaped by my experiences. The same went for my husband. He had set routines in place for how he ran the household and dealt with the children. I had to come in and figure out where my place was in all of this.

For most of my life I suppressed my feelings. I was always the one to solve everybody else's problems. I was the one person that remained positive regardless of the situation. When I went to prison it was no different. I helped to start a women's ministry, taught business and life skills classes, even coached people. I never dealt with my real feelings and the reality of my situation. Therefore, upon coming home, I was in a mental space of wanting to "do me." I felt like I had always done what everybody else wanted me to do for my entire life, that now it was my turn.

Now you know that frame of mind doesn't work when you are a wife and mother, especially when your husband has stood by you for three years while you were away and raised your children! My mentality was so backwards when I came home. I wanted to immediately re-start my business and focus on building an empire rather than making sure my family was mentally and emotionally healthy. Now don't get me wrong, I was there as a mother and wife, just not 100% fully mentally and emotionally present the way I should have been.

I had been defined by my business and my accomplishments. I was a high-achiever growing up and started my first company at 19. Hard work and commitment to my business was what I knew. Coming home to making $8.00 an hour was something I didn't know how to do. It took me a long time to just be ok with that. I was so used to making money that it was a hard adjustment for me. This caused such a huge strain on my marriage. My husband felt, and rightfully so, that I should have been more focused on really re-building our family and marriage. If you read a few sentences back you will notice that I used the word "my" a lot instead of "we" and "us." When I came home I really lost sight of the fact that it was about our family and not just my transitioning.

Life got better. Within the first year, I went from $8.00 an hour to a part-time consulting position at $1,750 per month. The progression from consulting to contracting work of $6,600 each month within two years, then to owning my own business generating over $10,000 month within three years. The rest is history. During this time, our marriage had its ups and downs, high-highs and low-lows. We wanted to expand our family. During this process I had two miscarriages within a six month time period and finally gave birth to our second son within two and half years of me being home. The miscarriages were very rough for me because I really didn't talk about them. I processed the pain internally and for a while, every time I saw someone pregnant I would break out in tears.

I wasn't really sure how to deal with it. I prayed a lot and read scriptures about multiplying and my seed being blessed. I didn't really get excited about my pregnancy with my youngest son until I was almost seven months pregnant, because I wanted to make sure I wasn't going to experience another disappointment.

This journey of finding love, being separated from my family, to growing and learning has taught me the importance of always dreaming and believing. Throughout this process I always felt like there was something greater in store for my life. Even though I was in a relationship that ultimately lead me to prison, I can look back to find all of the positive things in it. I am able to look back and gain wisdom from so many of the bad choices and decisions that I made. This journey has taught me to believe in true love and know good men are out there. Even though society says there are no good black men, I am here to tell you that there are.

Being in prison taught me that you are stronger than you think. I remember telling my girlfriend many years ago after she had a miscarriage, I could never go through that. Low and behold I had two! With God's help I made it through. You never know what hand you are going to be dealt in life. All you can do is just take it one day at a time. I remember many nights when I was at the camp wondering how long this was going to last, praying for God to give me an early release.

Every time the church doors opened I was there. Every time there was a revival, I was there. Every time the news had a broadcast about reducing federal prison sentences, I was watching. However, God didn't deliver me from it; He gave me the strength to go through it.

I am absolutely the wife, mother and business owner that I am today because of those experiences. They humbled me and exposed me to people of all walks of life. It increased my patience, perseverance and definitely my compassion. They also taught me that the seeds you sow, will reap a harvest. Joyce Meyer said, "You will reap what you sow, but not necessarily where you sow." That is so profound to me because I believe that many of the seeds that I sowed in my previous relationship resulted in the harvest that I have today as my husband. Don't get weary about not seeing the harvest where you planted the seeds rest assured the harvest will show up in your life and most times when you least expect it.

A Time of Reflection

When I look back at my life while I was away from my family, it truly seems like I am on the outside looking in at someone else's story. Today, I feel so far removed from it. I often sit back and ask myself how has our marriage survived? I know without a shadow of a doubt that the top two reasons were God and the strength of my husband. I was really in a very emotional and unhealthy state when I met my husband, of course I didn't know that at the time. I had just come out of a very mentally and verbally abusive relationship; I was facing legal challenges, and truly had no idea of who I was. I brought tons of baggage and wrong thinking into our marriage which didn't allow us to start off with a strong foundation. In retrospect, I was in no position to be getting married or having a child. My first priority should have been getting my head together and figuring out what I needed to do for my life.

I asked my husband why he feels our marriage survived when 70% of African American households are run by single parents. He gave me two answers: (1) God and (2) his maturity. He was very candid with me and said that if we had met several years prior to when we did, our story probably would have turned out a lot different. My husband had gone through a divorce and saw the effects that it had on our daughter. He didn't want to repeat that cycle again with our children. Therefore, he placed the needs of our family first even when he wasn't receiving what he needed physically, emotionally or mentally from me.

Another question I asked my husband was if he could go back and make different decisions what would he change? I answered that question for him and said not marry me. Seriously, he said that he would be more deliberate about taking care of himself mentally, emotionally and spiritually versus relying on the marriage to provide him a place of comfort and emotional stability. What I understand now, that I didn't understand then, was that I cannot give to my husband what I don't possess myself.

The Three Biggest Lessons I Have Learned Throughout This Process

- Lesson #1 - One of the most important lessons that I learned throughout this process is that you cannot give to someone what you don't have.

225

When I came home, my husband expected me to fall right into the role of being a wife and mother. He had traditional values of what that meant for him. The only problem – I didn't know who in the heck I was. I wasn't able to step into the roles that he wanted because I was still trying to define who I was and what I wanted for my life.

It is very difficult to go through the self-discovery process when you are married with children. They have needs, wants, and desires that they expect for you to fill. However, if you are an empty vessel, how can you pour into someone else? If I could go back and do things differently, I wouldn't have made false and empty promises to my husband or myself. I would have gone to counseling and worked through past issues that I had to really set me up on a journey for great success. It is difficult to work things out in your own head; most times it requires the help of someone else whether it is a coach, counselor, or friend.

- Lesson #2 – God has to be in control of your marriage and your life. I know without a shadow of a doubt that if God was not the head of the lives of both my husband and me, we would be divorced and I would be a single parent. I was so out of order for many years in my marriage. I was disrespectful, most times without knowing it and really selfish, also not really knowing it. Now, I'm not a confrontational person so when I say disrespect, I am not talking about yelling, cursing and fighting. I am talking about not listening to what my husband needs and providing it.

I was so focused on "me" that I wasn't able to hear what he was saying. If I could go back and have a do-over, I would make sure that my priorities were in order from the beginning. My priorities use to be business, my children, business again, my husband somewhere down the list and I wasn't even on the list. I would have made sure that my priorities were myself – meaning my relationship with God and self-care – my husband, my children and then the business. I would have prayed more and trusted God more. I would have listened and talked less. One valuable thing I learned is that I would rather be happy than right.

Simply put, I don't always have to say something, silence can sometimes be golden. Most importantly, I would have let go and let God. I would not have tried to push so hard with my business, I would have trusted God's timing for what he wanted to do with my family and business, being more patient.

- Lesson #3 – You have to respect and build your husband up. Oh my goodness, how can I expect my husband to be loving and adoring to me if I disrespect him and not build him up? I truly wish I would have truly gotten this lesson 10 years ago. I was tearing my husband down and not even realizing it. The words that came out of my mouth and the actions or better yet my non-actions were having a tremendous effect on my husband. I was so tapped-into my masculine energy because I am very assertive in my business that I was bringing that energy home and not really stepping into my femininity. It was more like I was competing against my husband versus complimenting him. I had to learn that my individual goals could not conflict with the vision that my husband had for our family. If I won and my husband or children lost, then the team still lost. I had to shift my mind from being focused on just my goals and focused on the higher vision of our family.

One important component of this was making sure that my husband's needs were met and realizing that I am the help meet and not the other way around. I was expecting my husband to adjust to me versus me adjusting to him. Whew baby, that was a very sobering process to really understand this lesson. In fact, I am still a work in progress in this area. If I could wave my magic wand, go back and change some things. I would be more submissive to my husband. Yes, I said it more submissive. Please don't put the book down (he..he...), keep reading.

Since my husband is a man of God and has a great heart for his family I would listen to him more and let him lead our family without resistance. I would give my input, however, if he made decisions that I didn't agree with for our family. I wouldn't fight him on it, I would just pray about it. What I have learned is that if I give whatever it is to God, it will always work out just like it is supposed to.

I've also learned that when I am in a place of submission to my husband he is also submissive to me in my areas of strength. The bible says submit yourselves one to another. Since I am strong in business, those are areas that he can refer to me and vice versa. However, if I am out of order and not being a help-meet then the house and family is out of order. Before, you get your panties in a wad, my life and business have always experienced the most success when I am in alignment with my family and marriage. When I honor those things that God has blessed me with in my life, he honors and blesses everything that my hands touch. Do it, and see what happens.

The Three Biggest Lessons My Husband Learned

This section will be way shorter than mine because my husband gets straight to the point. These are the top 3 things that he has learned:

- Lesson #1 – Don't allow someone else's words to affect the destiny of your life even if it is your wife.

- Lesson #2 – Let God have a presence in your life and marriage. Don't immediately react based on your initial emotions. Most time, reacting to your initial emotions isn't the best decision.

- Lesson #3 – When you are a husband and father you have to place the well-being of your family above what you want to do, even when you don't feel like it.

Life isn't always going to be neat and easy. Sometimes it is messy, inconvenient and uncomfortable. Be thankful where you are because it could always be worse. When I start being ungrateful, I think back about the lonely nights missing my husband and kids and not being able to do one thing about it. Freedom was so close, yet so far and out of my reach. The bad thing about it was, I didn't have physical or mental freedom. I was bound up all the way around and didn't even know it.

A lot of times your purpose will be birthed out of your pain and the most difficult times in your life. In my darkest valley is where I really discovered my love for teaching and coaching. What I know for sure is if you have breath, you have all that you need to create the life that you desire.

Living a happy and abundant life is not just about money. It is about peace, loving yourself and no longer being held hostage by your past. Isn't it time for you to take a step forward to accomplish your dreams? Make a decision today to pursue your passions and purpose which will ultimately lead you to profits. Remember to Live Your Authentic Life!

Flesh, Blood and Tears: Murder in the Worst

DEVAY CAMPBELL

. . . .

The Early Years

David was my younger brother and best friend. As far back as I can remember, we did everything together. We laughed and daydreamed; played dolls and climbed trees. Being with him gave me a sense of comfort, of belonging, and that's something I'll always be grateful for. I'm not sure why we were so close, I just know we were.

We grew up in a single-parent home where my mother worked second shift in the medical field. In case you don't know, second shift is the absolute worst shift on earth for a parent because it means leaving the kids alone usually between 3 p.m. and 11 p.m. I'm sure my mother didn't want to do it, but second shift paid more money. Besides, when you think about it, hospitals can't make exceptions just because a person has children. People get sick—especially at night, and I suppose someone has to be there.

I was okay with her having to leave us though, because it meant I was growing up. Being thirteen was a big deal to me. I was now a teenager *and* I finally had the chance to stay at home alone without a babysitter. The only downside, if there was one, was that I realized I needed a lot of guidance myself. Plus, David and I were so close that he saw me as a friend and not as someone he had to listen to. But like older siblings in my situation, I had no choice and I played my role well.

David did not give me problems except when I would tell him he could not go outside until he completed his math homework. He hated math and would try everything including telling me he did not have homework. We knew calling my mother at work was a no no and meant one or both of us would be in trouble.

"Do your homework," I told him. "Get your side of the room clean," I said, because we shared a room for a long time so we had sides. "Sure, it's okay if you go outside now," I would smile. There is a certain magic to being a big sister. You're childless, but you have a child; at least that's how it feels. You have a little one; someone you're responsible for, someone who depends on you to guide them, discipline them. Well, siblings usually don't like the discipline part; it has to be done when necessary! And set a good example.

Yes, despite being only two-and-a-half years older than him, I felt responsible for my brother. But more important than that, I had fun doing what I did for him. Somehow his easy-going personality just made it all so easy.

We probably could have gone on like that forever, but...I got pregnant. That's right, I got pregnant during my sophomore year in high school at the age of 15 and suddenly went from a carefree girl with her life in front of her, to an unwed mother who couldn't hide what she'd been doing. It was the most embarrassing, isolating, and toughest time of my life. "How could this happen? What are you going to do now? How could you do this to your mother?" I heard this from every single person in my life who felt they were entitled to an opinion and that I was obliged to listen.

Everybody gave me an ear-full, everybody except David. He never judged me. I was pretty sure he was disappointed in me, but he never said a word. If he thought I had messed up my life, he didn't say anything about that, either. However, I do think he knew I was disappointed in myself. After all, I had received a big fat "F" as a role model. Yet, whatever he knew, whatever he felt, he said nothing, and his silence meant everything.

When the baby came, David accepted her with open arms. "I'm an uncle," he smiled as he held her close and did all the things uncles do...cuddled her and rocked her back and forth. He stepped right into his role. In fact, his enthusiasm over her reminded me of how I felt when I took care of him while our mother worked. When she cried, he took pride in calming her down by walking through our tiny apartment.

During my senior year of high school, there was an hour-and-a-half gap between the time my mother left for work and I came home from school. The baby needed a sitter, but David knew we couldn't afford it. "I'll do it," he volunteered. And he did. At 13 years old, he gave up the time he normally played basketball and hung out with his friends just so he could make my baby smile at his silly, off-key songs and his funny peek-a-boo games. It was more than sweet. And it was also a load off my shoulders.

Looking back, I realize now that our roles reversed as we got older. David – my baby brother – grew into the "big", little brother. Even my mother began to see him differently. "You're the man of the house," she would say. And he was, he really was. Whenever we returned home after dark, before he'd let my mom and I go in, he went inside to check things out. He was that protective. If his friends inquired about dating me, he would tell me about it, but quickly follow up with two or three reasons why they really weren't good enough for me. He would also warn me to stay away from the high crime areas of town.

My brother was six-feet-three-inches tall, towering over my mom and me. I felt safe when my baby brother was around. I smile even now as I remember that some of his friends called me his little sister, even though I was more than two years older. And he didn't correct them either; he would just try to shut me up when I did.

By the time we were young adults, our bond was even stronger. We would talk for hours on the phone, and I often refereed his disagreements with his girlfriends or our mother. We also had a standing date on Mondays. "Ready for your 'all you can eat crab legs'?" he would ask like he didn't already know the answer. "Can't wait," I always said. Then, we would meet at our favorite restaurant and act as silly as we had when we were children. That meant the night was filled with corny jokes, or if something serious happened in the world, then one of our thought-provoking exchanges about rappers, sports, life and death. We would comment, out-talk each other and debate like only true friends can do. Many times we ended up agreeing to disagree, and then we'd tell each other how much we were looking forward to the next time. Yes, he was my very best friend. The fact that he was my brother was just icing on the cake.

Weightlifting? Really?

One day while visiting David at his girlfriend's home, where he spent many nights, he made me aware of an injury he sustained while lifting weights. I couldn't believe he was lifting weights, or exercising at all, for that matter, but that was his story. I was interested to see what he was talking about. When he lifted his arm I was shocked! His armpit protruded underneath his skin. I did not believe something like that could be caused by lifting weights. I was immediately concerned, but he made so many jokes about it that I eventually loosed up and joined in poking fun.

My mother was in another room and I asked her to come into the kitchen to examine this weightlifting injury. The look on her face told me she did not find our jokes funny. Even though she works in an administrative capacity in the medical field, she is pretty sharp as it pertains to most things medically related. "I'm making you a doctor's appointment," she told him, and she did so the very next day.

On the day of the appointment, I remember glancing at the clock at about 10:55 a.m., and I thought to myself that David's appointment time was near. After work, his girlfriend and I planned to go shopping and hang out, but she didn't answer when I called at 5:30 pm. I then called my mother to see how the appointment had gone, but could not reach her either. Now, not reaching either of them was very odd and made me feel a little uneasy.

I went back and forth, calling the two of them, then David's girlfriend finally answered. "Are we still going out?" I asked. "I don't feel like it," she said. Her voice was very low and she sounded as if something was wrong.

"What's wrong?" I asked.

"I will let your mother explain," she said. Her answer shocked me, yet I wasn't truly surprised, given my gut feeling. That reply, as simple as it was, told me everything I needed to know.

"Does my brother have cancer?" I asked. I don't know why I asked, but I did. I waited for her answer. She could not speak. She just began to sob into the phone and refused to give me an answer at first. I think she finally mumbled something that sounded like, "Yes." That's when I hung up the phone and drove to her home as fast as I could.

It was one of those moments where you arrive at a place, but you don't remember exactly how you got there. I didn't remember passing certain landmarks, stopping at red lights, or anything. My mother met me at the door. My aunt and dad arrived a few minutes after I did. Everything seemed so...different, because it had been a while since we were all in the same place at the same time. The scene looked serious—it *was* serious.

You see, a week earlier, my brother had been healthy, in good spirits, and making fun of his pulled muscle/weightlifting injury. But on this day, he was in bed and in the fetal position with a blank stare on his face. He didn't even acknowledge his host of visitors. As for me, I didn't know what to say or do to make it better. I just stood and looked at him feeling helpless.

Thankfully, my aunt, the Christian matriarch of the family, stepped in and saved the day. She arrived with her bible and began to lighten the mood.

My aunt had been in a situation like this before when my grandmother passed away. Her children were all young adults when she passed, and my aunt stepped right in to take care of her siblings, nieces, nephews, and her own children. She did a great job, too. You could always depend on her for a good meal and the good word. I could see it was going to be like that in this situation, too.

"Remember," she told my brother, "that David in the bible was an overcomer. Not only do you share the same name with him, you have the same spiritual power!" David's mood brightened a little and he seemed to respond to her message. In fact, everyone in the house was in a better place, including me. I needed something to ease my mind and put a positive spin on this situation. Her words certainly helped. I left feeling much better. Still, we all knew there would be tough times ahead.

I couldn't help but question how a nineteen year old, healthy male could end up with cancer. After all, I was usually the sickly one. I was the one who always caught colds and anything the wind blew my way. David, on the other hand, was the picture of health. The only two ailments I ever remember him having were pink eye and chickenpox in elementary school. That's it! Cancer felt like a death sentence to me. I wanted to think positive and believe the best, I really did, but I couldn't help allowing myself to think about what it would be like with him.

In the days that followed, I read everything I could on his diagnosis: Hodgkin's Lymphoma. I found out it was cancer of the lymph nodes. In the meantime, David had chemotherapy every Friday for months, and surgery to remove the mass from under his arm, which was followed by radiation treatments. It was a tough time for him, but it was a tough time for me, too. I couldn't imagine losing him.

One saving grace was that he didn't get sick or lose his hair. And that sense of humor of his was still intact. He grew closer to the church and he also got baptized. One day we debated about a decision I made.

"I am an organ donor," I said.

"Why do you want to spread your organs around?" he asked me, and further clarified his question. "When I pass away, I want my soul to be at rest." He didn't think I would be at rest if my organs were in other people. Yes, these conversations were morbid, but we still had them...and often. I was even more sensitive to these talks because he had cancer.

One day, at the end of his cancer treatments, David and I were riding and had a long talk about life and death. "I'm not afraid to die," he said. These simple words shook me up so badly that I became very emotional. I searched for any words that would soften him and make him change his mind. "But you have so many people to live for," I said, yet he stood his ground. He was not afraid to die and that was that. I tried to hide my feelings but...he was my brother and he knew me well. It was obvious that I was sad. In fact, I was so upset by the conversation, I decided to end the ride early.

June 9, 1997 we had a date to eat crab legs as usual. The only difference in this date was that it was to celebrate my birthday which was the day before. I had decided I would try to meet a little later than we usually did since he often complained that I ate too early. Of course, I complained that he ate too late, but on this particular day, we decided to compromise.

The problem was we didn't notify each other. So when I arrived to pick him up, he said he waited for me as long as he could and had already eaten. He did offer to pay for my solo crab leg meal, which was $21.99, and since I was turning twenty four years old he gave me $24. As I walked away with my crab leg money, he called me back and gave me another dollar. "This extra dollar is for the next year," he smiled. Since I didn't want to eat crab legs without him, I grabbed something to go and headed home.

The Incident

The day was Saturday, December 6, 1997 – I will NEVER forget that date. I was visiting my aunt, the Christian matriarch, and had a great day, but that night I became ill. She didn't want me to drive home so she asked me to spend the night with her to give myself time to recover. I had packed up my daughter and decided to drive home, but she insisted. I decided she knew best, so my daughter and I got out of the car and spent the night with her.

On Sunday morning, at 10:00 am, I recall my aunt waking me up with the question, "How does my outfit look?" I gave her a sleepy nod and went right back to sleep. The next thing that woke me up was the phone ringing. And ringing. The person on the other end just would not hang up so I finally answered it. After all, it was noon and I needed to get out of the bed. It was my mother, and initially she was stunned to hear my voice instead of my aunt's. Then she continued talking and she spoke the words that changed my life.

"Tell your aunt to meet me at the hospital," she cried. "Your brother's been shot!" She told me that the shooting took place at the BP Gas Station on Liberty Street and her husband's son was the shooter. Shot! I was totally caught off guard. A part of me didn't believe it, but my pounding heart and racing thoughts were a reality check.

I did as my mother asked and called the church my aunt was visiting that day. Since it was different from her normal church home, I had to explain what she was wearing in order for them to know who I was talking about. When she came to the phone I delivered the news, and then called a ride to pick me up. I couldn't drive myself; I was too emotional and knew I was going to need support. I dropped my daughter off with a trusted friend and went to be by my brother's side.

On the way to the hospital, my friend drove past the gas station where the shooting occurred. I'll tell you, the sight of the yellow police tape made my crying go from five to ten in no time. I automatically assumed the tape was a sign that someone had been killed. My friend read my mind and tried to calm me. "I'm sorry for driving in this direction," he said. "And just so you know, the police put up the tape to secure the scene for evidence. It doesn't mean anything." I wanted to believe him. Just hearing those words made me feel much better, even if my breaking heart secretly knew the truth.

As it turns out, the guy who shot my brother was my mother's husband's son. If I had known him better, I might have called him my stepbrother, but I had only seen him twice before this horrible incident. He lived in the same community as my brother's girlfriend, David knew him better than I did. This, coupled with the fact my brother and he were close in age and both males, had added to their bond. They played video games together and even started referring to one another as brothers. So I don't think anyone could have predicted that these two guys would end up as enemies.

My friend dropped me off at the emergency room door while he went to park. I jumped out of the car running into the hospital. I didn't recognize anyone in the waiting room. I stopped abruptly and then moved toward the triage nurse. "Is David Campbell still there?" I asked. I was hoping with everything I had that she would say no, but somehow I knew better. She had the security guard escort me to a separate room, and when I went through the door, I saw it was occupied by my mother, her husband, one of his sons, and his nephew.

I probably don't have to tell you that I was uncomfortable being around my mother's husband at that moment. I did not care for him *before* this incident, but now the thought that we were in the hospital on a Sunday because his son had shot my brother really sickened me!

My aunt arrived, followed by my uncle. Both very upset, and their frustration was aimed directly at my mother's husband. In fact, they were so loud hospital security decided to divide us into two separate groups. I was with my mother, her husband, his son, and his nephew. The other group consisted of my brother's girlfriend, who was a close friend to me by then, even though we didn't start out that way, and my uncles, aunts, cousins and friends who had received the news and came to the hospital.

I understood the reason for the division, but I was as neutral as Switzerland. I felt it really wasn't fair to isolate myself from the others and I was torn. My mother needed me at that time, but I didn't want to be forced to stay in the same room with her husband. I know it sounds strange, however I didn't want him to have the pleasure of seeing me hurt and in pain. I would have felt free to cry in the company of my other family members and my brother's friends.

Under the circumstances, you would think he would have offered a word of encouragement or at least would have expressed his sorrow. Was that really too much to ask? But he didn't give anything, so I didn't want to give him anything either.

I paced the room and kept my pain hidden behind a mask of calmness. It was just my way. I was known for and took pride in being emotionally tough. There were not many situations in life where I allowed myself to be emotionally vulnerable. This was one of them. Knowing that, it was a good thing that I cried all the way to the hospital because now my heart and mind and body were aching, but I wouldn't let it out. I was scared and confused. I wanted to just let go and scream, but I was trapped in room with someone I did not want to see me weak. Damn! And to add insult to injury, *his* son was responsible.

We waited for hours. The hospital staff checked in from time to time to notify us that David was in surgery. I spent my time pacing and plotting. What I mean is, I began to wonder how to use my employee ID badge to try to gain access to where my brother was. I might have forgotten to mention, that this hospital where I happened to work part time. My ID was a high-access badge, and it was inside my purse. Could I use it to see David?

It seemed like a good plan, but I must have forgotten about the security guard who followed me everywhere, including when I went outside to get some fresh air. No, I wouldn't be able to break protocol to see my brother. At this point it was apparent that delusion had set in. The closet-sized room we waited in for at least four hours seemed to get smaller and smaller by the minute.

Then finally! A doctor approached who looked like he was bringing news. As he got closer, the look on his face did not appear to being good news. My heart started beating too quickly! I turned my back to him and grabbed the phone, foolishly thinking that if I called someone, anyone, I didn't have to hear what he had to say. I thought I could delay the inevitable.

Regardless of my actions, he had a message to deliver and that is what he did. "We tried to save him. A bullet pierced his heart." Those were his exact words. What? In my heart I knew what he was going to say, but to hear that my brother was murdered floored me. It literally and figuratively floored me. I don't remember collapsing, but the next thing I knew, my eyes were closed and I could hear the voices around me.

After I was helped to my feet, I rushed out of the room and out of the hospital doors. "I don't want to be here," I said to myself. It was true. I did not want to be in the hospital and I definitely did not want to be a part of the world without my brother. By then, my family and my brother's girlfriend caught up to me. Someone gave them a wheelchair and they were trying to force me into it. I refused, then walked back into the hospital.

Our family begged them to let us see him and they refused. I thought this was strange. Although this was my first experience with something so tragic, I remembered seeing TV shows where the family had to identify the body. All I know was that we wanted to see him. That didn't happen. I really don't remember anything else about that experience.

I left the hospital in denial. After all, they said he was gone, but I didn't actually see him, right? I slept in my brother's bed that night. I wanted to feel close to him, but that was a mistake. It was not a restful sleep at all. Whenever I closed my eyes, I saw images of his face with tears streaming, and other disturbing images. His girlfriend also slept in his bed with me. She wanted to feel close to him too. It was one of the worst nights of my life. I woke up several times crying and coughing. I had so many questions, so few answers, and a heavy heart and racing mind.

Later, I learned that David had been shot at the gas station after a physical altercation with the shooter. The shooter had easy access to his home along a path leading to and from the gas station so it was quick and easy for him to go home to get a gun after the fight.

When he returned, David was in the car and leaving the scene. The shooter walked up beside the car and shot my brother three times. One shot hit him in the side, one hit him in the neck, and the other bullet struck him in the heart. According to the doctor, the bullet in the heart was the fatal shot.

The questions came flooding back. How did this happen? Just three weeks before my brother's 22nd birthday, one man with a gun had done what cancer couldn't do. He had taken David's life. Didn't he know that David was my friend, my brother, *his* step-mother's son, a dad, a friend an uncle and a nephew? Didn't he care? Did he think about any of that on his walk home to get the gun? Didn't he know that David's birthday was less than one month away and that he and I had many more crab legs dates to attend? If my brother had left the gas station just a few minutes earlier, he would have been gone when the shooter came back, and still alive. My mind raced out of control as I spent most of my time trying to make sense of what really was just a senseless act.

I was present to assist with funeral arrangements, casket decisions, and selecting his outfit. That was me; the big sister, making decisions for my baby brother just like I had when I babysat him so long ago. My mother valued and honored my decisions. This would be my one of the last things I could do for him as a big sister and it was empowering. Empowered or not, I was still taking it hard.

The days and weeks that followed overwhelmed me with grief. I spent a lot of time with my mother.

Unfortunately, her husband was often there. I tried to avoid him, but sometimes it just wasn't possible. To be honest, I didn't even want to look at him, I could not stay away from my mother though. I didn't trust him with her alone. It was obvious through his actions and comments that he didn't have our best interests at heart. My mother needed "inside" support. I was broken and grieving, too, still I tried to be there for her the best I could.

Meanwhile, my grief was noticeable to everyone. I sat for what seemed like days in one little spot on the couch. I sat there so much that my co-workers conspired with my mother to get me out of the house. "There's a mandatory meeting," they said. "Everyone has to be there." I refused to go. I know they didn't understand, but the word "mandatory" really didn't mean anything to me. You see, I was working two jobs at the time: I was a Life and Health Insurance Agent and a Registration Clerk. The Registration Clerk job was at the same hospital where my brother died. In fact, the lab I worked in was three doors down from the morgue.

Ironically, the life insurance company I worked for also insured my brother. Why in the world would I want to counsel others about and sell life insurance to people at time like this? It was too much. I didn't care to go back to work, even if they thought it was mandatory. Both jobs reminded me of my loss.

My mother finally persuaded me attend the "mandatory meeting." She did this by allowing me to wear one of her winter white pantsuit that I admired so much. It took everything I had, but I attended the meeting at the life insurance company's corporate office in Durham, North Carolina. The office was over an hour from my home, and on the way, my co-workers tried to make small talk and jokes. I was pissed. All of this was followed by lunch at my favorite soul food restaurant. I always did love a good meal, and they knew it.

Funny, but I can remember the lunch, yet I can't tell you what the meeting was about to save my life. While we were in the restaurant, my co-workers informed me that the meeting was actually not mandatory at all. They had been checking on my welfare after my mother had told them I would barely move out of the spot I had chosen to plant myself in. I have to admit, while I appreciated the gesture they made in getting me out of the house, I was very upset that they disturbed me.

All I wanted was to sit there and remember...nothing more. Even the happy thoughts and memories tortured me. My motivation level to do anything else was zero. The idle time didn't help. I was in this state for at least two months. Returning back to work and having a normal routine helped me to work through some of the depression and grief.

The Trial

Six months after the incident, the trial now loomed before us. Very soon my family and I would have to relive the pain of losing my brother all over again. This time, we would get to face the murderer in court. The District Attorney tried to offer him a second-degree murder plea deal, which he turned it down. I was glad he did. In my opinion, this was clearly a premeditated murder, which was grounds for a first-degree murder conviction, not second-degree. I wanted him to have his day in court.

I remember the night before the trial was very tough for me. I couldn't sleep, and cried off and on all night. It was like taking a few steps backward in the healing process. The morning of the trial was worse. It rained cats and dogs, and the walk into the courthouse seemed like it took an entire hour. That was because I walked as slowly as I could, even though the parking deck was right across the street.

Though I was looking forward to the closure, I hated that I was going to hear all the gory details of the worst day of my life being recounted. Prior to the trial, my mother shared some information that gave me at least some pleasure. "We are going to assist the District Attorney with selecting the jury," she said. My pleasure was mixed with a little anxiety. What if I selected the wrong people? What if they believed the murderer's story of self-defense, because that was what he was calling it. In the end, I felt that being directly responsible for putting the people in place that would hopefully send my brother's murderer away would be an honor. I put a little more pep in my step once I was actually inside of the courthouse.

Unfortunately, the day started off bumpy due to a verbal confrontation with the defendant's two sisters. I overheard them telling their own mother that the defendant was justified in his actions.

"He's going to walk free," they said. I tried to ignore their comments, I really did. I stood there fighting back tears and holding my tongue, but in the end they tossed the phrase "self-defense" around one too many for me. Then came the icing on the cake. "He did what God wanted him to do," they said.

At first I felt sad for their mother. She was losing her son too. After that ridiculous comment, my feelings quickly turned to an "I don't care", rage-filled attitude. I was mad as hell! At that moment, all bets were off! Before I knew it, I yelled at their mother, "That's right, you need to keep crying because your son is going to jail for a while."

They stopped talking and asked one of their friends who I was. Their friend, my mother's husband's other son and I had grown up together so he knew I was David's sister. When he told them, they called me every name in the book. There were obviously ready to fight and shared my rage-filled position. Their mother tried to calm them. I was in there solo. It was just me and my umbrella. I was ready to protect myself if needed.

I had to remember we were in the lobby of the courthouse and my family needed me to get through the trial. Hell, I wanted to get through the trial. Going to jail was not an option. It had been six months. I laughed, and continued to talk about how their brother would pay and that they should be prepared to visit him behind bars. After five minutes of exchanging insults, I walked into the courtroom with my head held high. I left them in the lobby cursing so loud that I could still hear them. They were still yelling when the rest of my family arrived. My mother said they taunted her, too. They didn't know it, but they had given me the boost of confidence I needed to pick the jury. I wasn't scared anymore. I looked forward to it.

Selecting the jury was an interesting process. I tried to dismiss everyone that I felt would be biased or too lenient. One lady in particular was a stay-at-home mom who had been married to a career pastor for 40 years. I couldn't help wondering, did she believe in an eye for an eye, or would she object to ruining two lives? I really wanted to dismiss her, but it was decided that we should keep her. I'm glad we did. I felt better once she gave me a comforting look when I looked her way. It may seem silly, but her look gave me security in her guilty vote. I felt that she understood and acknowledged my pain. Also, I turned toward her to shield myself from seeing my brother's shirt, which they held up in court.

It was the gray t-shirt he wore the day he was shot. I remembered that shirt. There was blood on it and it had been cut completely down the middle. That caught me off guard! Seeing it took my breath away. The blood on it and the condition of it made the struggle to save his life real to me. In my mind I could see the paramedics cutting it to have quicker access to the bullet wounds. I could see them rushing, trying to stop the bleeding all to no avail.

It's strange to me that I didn't get emotional as I studied the photos of my brother's corpse. They passed the pictures around to the jury, my mother, and me. I paid attention to where the bullets entered his body, and especially to the look on his face. He looked like he was sleeping. I felt sad, somehow also relieved. It was the final piece of the closure I needed. In a way, this gave me more closure than his funeral. I guess that's because the funeral had happened so fast after the shooting, I was still in denial.

A few witnesses took the stand and explained how laid back and nonviolent my brother was, but the defendant was described as quite the opposite. Even his own mother explained that my brother was always nice. She painted a negative picture of her son and his lack of respect for her. I admit I respected her for telling the truth even though it was damaging to her son's reputation. Of course, no trial is complete without an expert witness who is ready to offer an expertly-crafted "disorder."

All of the cries for "self-defense" and all the attempts to make it seem like David deserved what happened to him fell completely flat. Nothing the defense said to discredit my brother and ruin his character worked on the jury, and I was so proud of that.

There was one huge road block in the trial. The only witness that was impossible to track down just happened to be the key witness. He was the passenger in the car with David that day, and was the only person to have seen the defendant go home and return with the gun. Everyone else had only heard what happened or was otherwise indirectly involved. We needed him at the trial, but he was nowhere to be found. I had even called his uncle, a local pastor to solicit his help. I called and visited anyone else that I thought could help us find him, and the detectives placed a warrant out for his arrest so he could be detained and be escorted to the trial. Despite all of the efforts, he was never found. Not then and not to this day, at least not that I'm aware of.

His absence left me nervous about the outcome. I found the strength to remain positive. All I knew was that I could not deal with the heartache of seeing the murderer walk free, or to see him to get a simple slap on the wrist. Because the key witness' absence changed our leverage greatly, we decided to offer the defendant a plea bargain on day three of the trial. It was the same plea bargain he had refused early on. After all, we wanted a first degree murder conviction and he wanted a self -defense charge. In the end, he was charged with second degree murder and discharging a firearm into an occupied dwelling which was the car. He was sentenced to over 24 years in prison.

I was overjoyed. It wasn't ideal, but it was better than the alternative, which was only time served. I wanted him to receive at least a year in prison for each year of my brother's life 21 years.

Overcoming the Pain

In the days and weeks following the trial, my emotions were up and down. I spent most of my time shifting between anger and hurt. The denial phase was definitely over. The realization that David, my beloved baby brother, was gone and not returning was a hard pill to swallow. I slowly developed a routine that was somewhat normal, but I still operated with a huge void and hole in my life. My best moments were spent reminiscing about some of the times I had with David, or spending time with my daughter.

One day I had a dream. David was in it. "I'm okay," he said. "I am just listening to music up here." This was such an epiphany for me. David and I had a mutual love for music. He was listening to music? Wow! For me, this meant he was telling me that he was doing something he enjoyed. I recalled how we often took rides to listen to new CDs or to have debates about which artist we liked the best. After the dream I knew I had to make a change.

In a weird way, I had felt that if I enjoyed life too much this meant I wasn't honoring his life or acknowledging what happened to him. I felt like I was supposed to be sad. Added to that was the fact that I carried around the guilt of not being able to help him or save him. In my heart I had been entertaining the thought that if I had visited him that Sunday morning to show him our photos from Thanksgiving dinner, he would not have been at the gas station that day.

Suddenly, so many things were coming back to me. I thought about how he looked up to me, how strong he thought I was, and how often he complimented me on being driven. He had had a great deal of faith in me; so much that he had often encouraged me to mentor his girlfriend. That dream encouraged me to carry on as the person David had known me to be and expected me to be when he was alive. I finally understood that he would not want me to be sad and unmotivated. He would not want me to only barely exist. I finally looked past my pain. When I did, I realized, everything happened the way it was supposed to happen.

Yes, I have always thought things happen for a reason. Of course, it is hard to think that way when the event is painful. The fact that my brother David had blessed the food and led the family in prayer for the first time less than two weeks earlier on Thanksgiving was his special goodbye. I realize that now. And the extra dollar he gave me for my 24th birthday that he had intended for the following year, and the closeness my family had experienced after his cancer diagnosis, were meant to brace us for that horrible day and the possibility of losing him. Growing through this process taught me to remember:

1. When you are going through a loss or a tough time, give yourself permission to grieve. You don't really need permission, it is your right. Don't stifle your emotions and feelings for anyone, and don't be paralyzed by guilt. You will get through the pain, but you must go through the process.

2. After you lose someone you love, miss them and grieve, but make a decision to take little steps towards a normal life. If you were ambitious,

creative, witty, and loving before you lost them, find it in yourself to continue to be that person. The best way to honor their life is to live yours so that they will be proud.

I truly believed that. And if I believe those things, then I must also believe that there was nothing I could have done to stop my brother from dying. I know that his death was premature and it happened way too soon for me. I also know I loved him and would never be ready to lose him. The point is...I understood it was not my guilt to carry.

Life and death happens when it is supposed to. I know now that honoring David's life and enjoying my own life are one and the same. To honor him, I laugh, I dream, I am motivated, I forgive, I laugh, I listen to music and dance; and I make a conscience effort to live unapologetically.

IN CLOSING ·

*I*t is my most sincere hope that you have enjoyed reading this anthology of women who were courageous enough to become ambassadors of Emotional Nudity and share their stories of faith, fear and fortitude. This project started out as a simple idea that blossomed into collection of stories then converted into a series of uniquely inspiring experiences.

As I sit back and breathe a sigh of relief, I am overcome with emotion and I am humbled by this finished work, but mostly I am grateful to the Almighty God for sending me every person who touched this book in the spirit of love and collaboration. I always tell my community, we are strong individually, but collectively we are an unstoppable power.

My dream is that his project will inspire, empower and transform those who read it and in some cases it will allow someone else to give birth to her own story. And for those you find the courage, here's to the power of YOUR chronicles.

Nakedly Yours,

Jai Stone | EMOTIONAL NUDIST & MASTER BRAND COACH

MEET THE AUTHORS

JAI STONE

Jai Stone is a Master Brand Coach based in Atlanta who is known as much for her "in your face" commentary as for her marketing prowess. Most frequently referred to as the Emotional Nudist, Jai helps women business owners to build profitable businesses without compromising their quality of life. Jai's raw and authentic approach to business and life is a magnet to other like-minded women who find healing and relief in removing their masks and living out loud without fear or apologies.

Connect with Jai at jaistone.com

@JaiStone

FELICIA PHILLIPS

• • •

Felicia Phillips designs results-oriented strategies that gives high-impact, peak performance, and increased profits for businesses for more than 20 years. Her desire to create economic opportunities for Entrepreneurs allows her to produce conferences that attract women around the world. As Founder of a global initiative, PINKtech, centered in economic empowerment and technology, Felicia's mission is to teach women how to leverage technology in their careers and businesses.

Connect with Felecia at www.feliciaphillips.com

 @thepinkmogul

MEOCHIA CLAYTON

* * *

As a result of her love for traveling, Meochia Clayton opened her own travel company, My Times Travel Agency. With her love of travel, she gives back through the efforts of her non-profit organization formed in 2014, Cruising with Autism, Inc. Having a son with autism, she works to provide cruise, resort, and recreational activities to children, teenagers, young adults, and families living with autism.

Connect with Meochia at www.cruisingwithautism.org

 @autismcruises

TOMIKA M. BROWN

* * *

Currently an Instructional Content Facilitator, Tomika Brown has a deep desire to help children in poverty break the cycle and teach them to understand they can be the author of their own success story. She earned a Master's Degree in Education Administration and is a freelance Education Journalist previously featured in The Movement Magazine. She currently resides in North Carolina with her supportive and encouraging husband and three children.

Connect with Tomika via @IamTomikaMBrown

TAMEKA L. WILLIAMSON

• • •

Tameka L. Williamson is an Executive Coach, Professor, Best-Selling Author, International Speaker and Trainer, and a member of the John Maxwell Team. Her passion is to develop and add value to people and businesses. She shares her struggles to help those plagued by the pains of their past to demonstrate they can loose the chains and transform their life into one with a high performing future.

Connect with Tameka at www.tamekawilliamson.com

 @IAmCoachTwill

TALISHA SHINE

* * *

Talisha is a 15-year IT software support professional and currently works for a global health service company. Also known as The Original Scope Scribe™ on Periscope, she leverages her love of tech and text in the live streaming social media arena. She obtained a Bachelors of Science in Computer Information Systems and Masters of Business Administration from DeVry and Keller Graduate School of Management. She currently resides in Northern Virginia with her daughter.

Connect with Talisha on 🐦 @ScopeScribe

MALLA HARIDAT

• • •

Whether she's training social and entrepreneurs how to run successful enterprises that educate, empower and support others as CEO of New Designs for Life, Malla applies her knowledge and expertise across various industries delivering insightful and engaging professional and personal development programming. As founder of Mom and Daughters Inc., she advises aspiring mompreneurs and kidpreneurs on how to monetize their dreams, talents, and ideas.

Connect with Malla at www.mallaharidat.com

@mallaharidat

BRANDI STARR

• • •

Brandi Starr is a speaker, a Modern Marketing Strategist & Consultant. Her company, Cassius Blue Consulting, helps entrepreneurs who are overwhelmed by marketing and struggling to increase their revenue, to devise and implement a magnetic marketing strategy to attract leads, convert them and increase their bottom line. She is the mother and stepmother to five amazing children, and lives in Atlanta with husband Rod.

Connect with Brandi at www.cassiusblueconsulting.com

 @CassiusBlueCo

BECKY A. DAVIS

• • •

"Becky A. Davis is known as the "Chief BOSSpreneur™" for her ability to help women start and grow successful businesses. She is a straightforward coach that develops women into well-rounded business owners. As a speaker, she uses her practical, street-savvy style and fuses real-life stories with her conversational techniques to connect with her audience on an intimate, intense, and individual level. Becky is the president of MVPwork LLC, a coaching and consulting practice for entrepreneurs.

Connect with Becky at www.beckyadavis.com

 @bosspreneur

T. RENEE SMITH

. . .

T. Reneé is passionate about helping women-entrepreneurs do the work with her step-by-step systems for building a business model, attracting clients, and positioning a brand that allows them to earn more money and have more free time as they balance work, womanhood, motherhood, and wife-hood. She shows each client how to "Live Your Authentic Life" as a superstar business owner who rocks stilettos, sweats, and suits!

Connect with T. Renee at www.treneesmith.com

 @coachtrenee

DEVAY CAMPBELL

• • •

Devay Campbell is a certified Human Resources Professional, Targeted Selection Interviewer, and Founder of Career 2 Cents, a career coaching and advice company. She leverages her professional and personal experience to empower individuals and groups in the areas of interviewing, leadership, workplace success, conflict resolution, negotiating and more. Her straightforward and encouraging style has attracted advice seekers across the globe, including the US, India, Dubai and Africa.

Connect with Devay at www.devaycampbell.com

 @devays2cents

WE WANT TO HEAR FROM YOU!

Has this book has made a difference in your life?

The Ambassadors of Emotional Nudity
would love to hear about it.

Leave a review on Amazon.com!

VISIT OUR WEBSITE AT
www.HerChroniclesBook.com

* * *

CONNECT WITH US ON

f /HerChronicles

FOLLOW THE HASHTAG
#HerChroniclesBook

CPSIA information can be obtained at www.ICGtesting.com
Printed in the USA
LVOW10s1325071015

457316LV00019B/318/P